Forging an Educative Community

Dear Bob

With deep admiration and respect of your work with children to forge educative communities! Truly you are a keeper of the flame.

[illegible]

Oct 12 2004

COUNTERPOINTS

Studies in the Postmodern Theory of Education

Joe L. Kincheloe and Shirley R. Steinberg
General Editors

Vol. 126

PETER LANG
New York • Washington, D.C./Baltimore • Boston • Bern
Frankfurt am Main • Berlin • Brussels • Vienna • Oxford

Rosalie M. Romano

Forging an Educative Community

The Wisdom of Love, the Power of Understanding, and the Terror of It All

PETER LANG
New York • Washington, D.C./Baltimore • Boston • Bern
Frankfurt am Main • Berlin • Brussels • Vienna • Oxford

Library of Congress Cataloging-in-Publication Data

Romano, Rosalie M.
Forging an educative community: the wisdom of love, the power
of understanding, and the terror of it all / Rosalie M. Romano.
p. cm. — (Counterpoints; vol. 126)
Includes bibliographical references and index.
1. Teaching. 2. Storytelling. 3. Imagination in children. 4. Tolerance—
Study and teaching (Elementary)—Activity programs. 5. Homelessness—Study
and teaching (Elementary)—Activity programs. I. Title.
II. Series: Counterpoints (New York, N.Y.); vol. 126.
LB1027.R64 372.13—dc21 99-35393
ISBN 0-8204-4565-7
ISSN 1058-1634

Die Deutsche Bibliothek-CIP-Einheitsaufnahme

Romano, Rosalie M.:
Forging an educative community: the wisdom of love, the power
of understanding, and the terror of it all / Rosalie M. Romano.
–New York; Washington, D.C./Baltimore; Boston; Bern;
Frankfurt am Main; Berlin; Brussels; Vienna; Oxford: Lang.
(Counterpoints; Vol. 126)
ISBN 0-8204-4565-7

Cover design by Lisa Dillon
Cover photograph by Rick Fatica

The paper in this book meets the guidelines for permanence and durability
of the Committee on Production Guidelines for Book Longevity
of the Council of Library Resources.

Printed in the United States of America

Acknowledgments

To Barbara Waxman, Sharon Thornton, Lynn P., John, and Larry who have taught me deeply about love and wisdom. And to all my students who continue to help me gain understanding of the value of forging an educative community. A special acknowledgment to Mr. Greg and his class, the hope of our democratic society.

Table of Contents

Foreword

As I travel with Storyline course in different parts of the world, I find it fascinating to notice the way in which this approach connects with the work already being done by progressive teachers. Classroom activities, pre-Storyline, often seem very similar but exposure to a Storyline course creates a new and exciting dimension. The story form provides a structure and security for both student and teacher. The major principles of respecting the prior knowledge of the learner and of encouraging hypothesizing and research provide a framework that teachers find supportive and professional. They consider learning and teaching as a partnership of mutual respect. With this approach very sensitive issues can be explored as in the interesting example described in chapter 1.

Rosalie Romano beautifully describes this caring atmosphere in her in-depth study of the work being done in Mr. Greg's classroom. Here is a wonderful example of principles in action. Mr. Greg, who is obviously a fine intuitive teacher, uses the Storyline form to great advantage. Students feel free to discuss real feelings behind the characters that they have created. Mr. Greg has the "red thread," the design of the story, and knows where he wants to go with it. At the same time the students feel that it's *their* story. They have ownership of the characters and their interaction. This is the recipe for a high degree of motivation. It's a delightful story.

Mr. Greg's classroom in *Forging an Educative Community* stands in contrast to the "back to basics" mood of change in many countries where competition is encouraged and success is measured by test scores. School results are compared in league tables and teachers are more and more encouraged to "teach to the test" with increasing prescription of content. We seem to be moving away from caring communities of learning and more toward competitive classrooms that fit more with the business/ corporate modes. Is that how we want to prepare our children for the future?

I feel proud to have had a small part to play in the development of this work through my contact with both Rosalie and "Mr. Greg." They are to be congratulated on the ways in which they have implemented the ideas of this methodology. It gives me great pleasure to commend this book.

Steve Bell
Storyline Scotland
Kendrick House Barfly Station
Stirlingshire, Scotland, UK
http://www.storyline-scotland.freeserve.co.uk

Introduction

"What is honored in a country will be cultivated there." And how do we unthinkingly honor what is not of honor? Or pass over that which cries to be honored and is "not seen"?

I took Plato's words into schools where I taught, both public K–12 and private academies, and wondered to myself what this school I taught in (if I imagined it a country) did honor. As a new teacher many years ago, I learned two important unwritten rules. These rules have a controlling power over us as teachers, exercising their dominion over us, too often without our being conscious of their authority in all we do in our classrooms with our students.

The first rule that controls us is the perception of what must be covered and the lack of time to do it. Teachers are so taxed in the time and labor intensive act of teaching that there is a constant yearning for the silver bullet that will make learning interesting and students engaged. While willing to listen to a new approach or method, teachers want ideas (as an editor once told me) "down and dirty," fast and directly applicable to their classrooms. Teaching within the site we call school puts extreme pressures on teachers to perceive that there is never enough time to do all that the district, the community, the parents, nay, the state and nation expect us to do. Therefore, any new idea or approach or method must be seen as immediately relevant if it has any chance of being brought into the classroom.

This brings us to the second rule. School is structured for reproducing the status quo, not for growth and transformation of human lives. The structure of school while purporting to be a place for new learning of both content and skills, has built-in barriers that run counter to teachers' —and therefore students'—learning and thinking about new ideas. Any teacher reading this will recognize that feeling of needing to "cover" all the material, do all the paperwork, deal with the myriad interruptions throughout the class period, having to choose at lunchtime whether to bolt down some food and make a quick restroom stop, or just sit quietly in the room and miss out on adult company in the faculty room. As teachers we deal in the concrete reality of curriculum, schedules, and the great juggling act each day brings with our students, who are *never* the same from day to day. And in this milieu, we are expected to teach content, life skills, social skills, health issues, and more. Now with state standards and, in many states, high stakes proficiency tests, teachers are faced with teaching more prescriptively, in atomized ways, to satisfy or meet what the state deems as student achievement.

Forging an Educative Community: The Wisdom of Love, the Power of Understanding, and the Terror of It All was guided to birth after over two decades in K-12 and higher education classrooms. I gave myself the gift of time to finish my doctorate, challenging myself to keep alive those moments in my classrooms with students and connect those experiences with the theory I was reading. As teachers, we pride ourselves in dealing with the "real work" of teaching, leaving theory to those whom we see far removed from schools. That attitude is but a thin veneer below which seethes in various degrees a commitment to students' lives, to their well-being, and always to their learning. As teachers we live our theory, for we have no luxury of intellectual space made for us to reflect upon what we do. Many of us forge those spaces alone, or if we are blessed with fortune, with other colleagues with whom we can share ideas and reflections. For example, Critical Friends is a growing movement amongst teachers in the United States, a structured approach to discussion of a book or one's teaching shared between other teachers, "Critical Friends," who critique and offer ideas to deepen and enliven one's pedagogy. Usually, Critical Friends meet once or twice a month as an on-going group to consult about a lesson a teacher may present for improvement or to discuss a recommended book, such as Deborah Meier's *The Power of Their Ideas*. This continued, stable association among teachers provides powerful support for growth and reflection out of which emerges the theories that animate their work in the classroom. No teaching is accomplished anywhere at any time devoid of some theory. Theory is what we do and how we proceed to do it in our classrooms. All our actions flow from our theories of what teaching and learning is, whether those theories are implicit and unarticulated or conscious and articulated. We must make the pedagogical space to be critically conscious of it. Our theories are at work daily alongside of us as we teach, deeply internalized and active, just within our reach below the surface of our daily actions.

I wrote this book for teachers, parents, educators, and all who value the work of teachers in classrooms, in this country, and across the world. For the work of teachers in other countries, as in this country, is strikingly and profoundly similar wherever there is the place called "school." *Forging an Educative Community* seeks to publicly acknowledge and affirm the invisible dimensions of classrooms. In this instance, an intensive study of a third grade classroom illuminates the principles of educative communities, which are the same regardless of the age or level of the students. My adult graduate and undergraduate students in my university courses respond, resist, reflect, and realize in the ways these third graders in Mr. Greg's classroom did, gradually becoming aware of how each is a part of the community in the classroom.

Mr. Greg's third graders awakened to their connection to the homeless in the park, the homeless in their school district, the homeless in their city, the homeless of the city of Kobe, Japan. These woven connections were not taught in the traditional sense of the word, through a book on homelessness or a lecture on homelessness or a movie on homelessness. The point is that these connections would never have been "woven" at all had they been taught in an atomized, one time fashion. These woven connections between and amongst the third graders and their teacher were forged through invisible dimensions of the curriculum, not to replace the formal curriculum, but as an intricate part of it. How Mr. Greg does this is described in the first chapter, which I present as a case of what it might look and feel like to be part of the forging of an educative community. Diverse learnings take place before our eyes. I honor the learning of respect as much as the physics of earthquakes; I honor the learning of compassionate imagination that animates and motivates literacy. Compassionate imagination is a profound, inextricable part of what we mean by literacy. I honor the power of understanding not for the speed in which it is finally accomplished, but for the space and deliberative pace in which student sense-making is cultivated.

All this is to alert you, the reader, that what you are about to read is not "down and dirty" or "quick and easy" or anything near the hundreds of "how-to" books that flood the bookstores each year. They, too, have their place. *Forging an Educative Community* is meant to provide you with a close reading of how a class forges an educative community. The hope is that once experienced, you will understand how an educative community is accomplished, how all those invisible, often "distracting" details in a classroom are in fact the specific ingredients necessary for forging an educative community. This makes sense when we think of so many crucially important human dimensions that enrich us throughout our lives that are palpable, yet invisible entities. I share these components with you, these hidden dimensions of an educative community.

Part of the way Mr. Greg forges this educative community is through the use of the Storyline Method. This method accords well with his theory of teaching and learning, and he uses it with wisdom to study the topic of homelessness. Mr. Greg uses Storyline to provide the context within which he and his students can make explicit respect and the ways to develop and reveal respect to each other. This is a method that engages and sustains imagination, and Mr. Greg uses the opportunities that emerge to develop a particular kind of imagination: compassionate imagination. Sense-making is crucial to learning that is memorable, and Mr. Greg uses Storyline to maintain the deep contextual foundation out of which the children can make their links between their lives, their characters' lives, and the lives of those who are homeless.

Using Storyline, a structured, active approach to learning, students and teacher develop relations of trust, compassionate imagination, sense-making that foster a sense of belonging among the teacher and children. Relations predicated and built upon these dimensions are critical attributes to an educative community for they actually strengthen and deepen what is learned. We see mathematics and geography and literature and science integrated and connected as essential to learning about the topic of homelessness. Throughout the description in chapter 1, literacy skills of reading, writing, computation, reasoning, critical thinking, penmanship, spelling, phonics, and much more are interwoven through the children's responses to Mr. Greg's key questions (in Storyline these are called critical incidents). The learning is active and meaningful for the students, and, I argue, therefore memorable. No, this is not a silver bullet that solves our challenges as teachers, nor is it being offered as such.

To forge an educative community is very hard work because the teacher must reinvent himself or herself, acting deliberately against school experiences in K-12 and perhaps even experiences in teacher preparation programs at college or university. This is not easy work, nor is it fast. It forces us to become present, that is, alert and aware, of what we do, how we do it, and why we do what we do in our teaching. Critically questioning ourselves forces us to interrogate our pedagogy. By itself, this is uncomfortable for many, yet incredibly liberating, too, for it offers us options, not habits; reflection rather than reaction; responsibility instead of rote responses. Finding the courage to question our pedagogy affords a benefit that is unexpected. A teacher discovers that there are other ways to experience time, one of our most limited resources in schools. We see how everything we do in our classrooms is a construction that is moveable and permeable, only awaiting our act of choosing. We discover we can choose to view curriculum beneath and beside and above the formal written document, and begin to see how informal (the unhighlighted, unmarked aspects) curriculum, such as respect and understanding, are critical components of what and how our students learn. In seeing the curriculum from a critical pedagogical stance, we find we can reorganize it, not only as Mr. Greg did using Storyline, but as I know many teachers do using multiple approaches.

In the second half of this book, I point to aspects of the attributes of an educative community that I argue are critical to fostering growth, intellectual and social at least, that might transform our students, and in the process, ourselves. Throughout this book, I make important assumptions. Here is one of them: I see education and democracy as an engagement of the imagination, and as such, always in a state of being, a state of discovery leading to a new discovery. Growth leading to new growth within the interactions of the classroom. Always a teacher must consider the social interactions of her or his classroom, for within those interactions are seeds for what we need to teach. My other assumption is that all social interactions are educational in some way. We see this vividly in Mr. Greg's response to his students' attitudes and behaviors toward the homeless people in the park. This is the prompt he uses to teach through Storyline. His teaching invites reciprocity because he believes that reciprocity is an essential feature of learning to live together. In his classroom, Mr. Greg invites his students to discover their public selves and the nature of being in a democratic society. Democracy, we know, is made up of our individual beliefs, actions, attitudes, and behaviors. Where do we learn to become democratic citizens? One place could be in the public space called school. Depending on what we honor there.

Chapter 1

The Wisdom of Love—An Example of an Educative Communty

Background on the Homeless Storyline

As usual, the autumn day had turned from cloudy and overcast to soft rain. I walked into the bustle of the Honey Bear coffeehouse to meet Mr. Greg, a teacher in a city school who had invited me to participate with him and his third graders the next time he taught a Storyline.[1] We sat down with a cup of hot, fragrant herbal tea and wondered aloud what the topic of our Storyline might be. Mr. Greg looked back on a recurring situation that the children had been bringing into the classroom throughout the fall. Some of his third graders had been teasing, throwing things, and running away from homeless people who slept overnight on benches or under trees in a park near the school. Though he had spoken to the children in small groups and as a class, the children's attitude toward the homeless people remained negative and fearful. Mr. Greg was concerned by the children's behavior and with the often exaggerated and frightful stories that they told the rest of their classmates about "those people" in the park. To teach a Storyline on homelessness might help the children better understand the plight of the homeless, as well as diminish their fear of "those people." Storyline would also encourage the children to talk about their assumptions and attitudes about homeless people, which we could then use to promote open discussion about their feelings and beliefs about homelessness. Posing a problem brought by the children themselves, especially using the discussion-based Storyline, would afford a potential opportunity to share assumptions about people who we perceive are different than we are, a key issue in schools today.

Mr. Greg is a colleague who completed his doctoral work a few years back in social studies and the arts. I had encouraged him to take a week-long workshop to learn about Storyline when Steve Bell, one of the developers of Storyline from Jordanhill College, University of Strathclyde, Scotland, came to our city and taught a workshop in Storyline in June 1991. Storyline is an integrative methodology that is discussion based and Mr. Greg uses the strategy often with his students. Through repeated tries, Mr. Greg has come to a point where he writes his own Storylines, choosing topics the children bring to him through their conversation or actions (as in the case of their behavior toward the homeless) to explore in ways that allowed for them to share their ideas and beliefs within a respectful framework. Using art to create a frieze and characters, as well as myriad other representations on a topic, gives the children a freedom to say things through their characters they might not otherwise say at all. In the fall, for example, Mr. Greg had begun the year with a Storyline that used astronauts as the characters, our universe as the setting. The topic of space was exciting and interesting to his third graders, offering an opportunity at this start of school to get to know one another, to share what they knew about space and astronauts, and to weave their imaginative ideas into the narrative. But beyond the academic learning, the children gave voice to their feelings about being all together in the ship. Mr. Greg learned what the astronauts felt about being explorers, about the gains and losses of being an astronaut, about the anticipation and the fear of being in space. The children revealed a great deal about themselves in the first few weeks of school, learning together about living in space—and living together in the classroom. Near the end of the month, as the Storyline drew to a close, Mr. Greg made the analogy of their class being like astronauts exploring outer space, that learning was like going into the unknown and being ready for the unexpected.

The children had been asking to do another Storyline since before winter break. Now would be a good time to do the homeless Storyline, immediately after winter break when enthusiasm was high from vacation, but interest and energy for schoolwork usually lagged. Mr. Greg could use Storyline to ease the children back into the school routine and provide a space to examine hidden assumptions and feelings about the homeless. And so it was in the first week after winter break that I found myself getting ready to go back into a classroom of third graders, where I would remain as a participant observer for the two months Mr. Greg would lead them through a Storyline.

The School and the Classroom

"Wetland Elementary" is a public school in the city near a park with a lake. Children are bused in from the south end of the city as well as from neighborhoods from the north. Neighborhood children also attend the school, which meets the district guidelines for positive desegregation, with balanced numbers of the majority and the minority population enrolled. Mr. Greg's class of twenty-eight third graders represents children from a number of different ethnic and cultural groups. About a third of the class is classified as majority; the rest are minority. Mr. Greg is a white male teacher.

On a drizzly morning in early January, I walked into the Wetland school's main office to register, and was pointed to the entrance of the playground area where Mr. Greg had his portable. I recognized which of the two portables was Mr. Greg's by the artwork painted on the sides of the building. The class, he had told me, had decided on a design and then painted a mural all around the portable. Bright colors, big, open flowers, butterflies, and birds circled the portable's exterior walls, all at a child's height. I arrived early before school began to talk with Mr. Greg and become familiar with the classroom. Even without the children there, the classroom seemed to teem with life from the artifacts of the children's activity.

The first thing I notice is the west wall of the portable, offering the only windows and natural light in the space. A well-used couch is placed strategically beneath them for best light, in case you want to read. Off in the southwest corner under piles of children's work and projects, a large and battered oak teacher's desk, which also has the daily tools of a teacher, stapler, chalk, eraser, and pencils, nestles up to an old-fashioned standing gas-heater that is vented through the roof. Portables have not changed much from when I was in school, I think. The south wall is filled, every inch of it, with remnants of another Storyline completed in the fall. There is a group of astronaut characters who are located halfway up the wall, looking down on all of us from their perch in space. Each space suited astronaut has a name tag written next to him or her. Two computers sit on desks underneath the legs of three astronauts. Other examples of student work fill in the spaces on the walls opposite.

The east wall is the "front" of the room, at least, that is where the blackboard is. The date is written in white chalk. I can hardly see the entire blackboard for all the boxes and papers stacked up in front of it. One of the boxes seems to be a box to hold students' papers.

By the north wall, a piano is crammed next to the door, under a tall shelf. That wall has a blackboard, too, and the huge shelf above it is used for storage, creating a boundary, cutting off the view of anyone who might be sitting at a desk. Here under the storage shelf on the blackboard there is a little space where our homeless Storyline characters will be placed.

The first bell cuts into the quiet. Up a muddy path leading to the portable, children come traipsing up the six steps that lead to the door. Tumbling into the classroom, steaming from walking and running in the drizzle, some children gather around the piano. One of the children playing a tune is Kim, a blind girl in the class. Kim is telling the small knot of children gathered around her the name of the piece she is playing. She tries to explain the words that go with the tune. Percussive notes from the piano pound out the rhythm of the song.

Some children pass by the box in front of the blackboard, placing papers in it, assignments due from yesterday, one child tells me. Still others come into the room, barely registering the singers and player at the piano, and make a beeline to the computers at the south wall. Soon a group of children is kibitzing around a peer who is engrossed in a computer game of Carmen San Diego. Parents are still leaving a couple of children off at the door, or the children have just had their daily bus ride to school. A child has lost something and has involved other students to look for the item by rummaging through desks and in nooks and crannies of the room.

The old wooden floor is warped and creaks, but no one notices, not even the furball of a white bunny hopping around the room, weaving in and around children's legs. The last bell rings, and the children rush to be in their seats before it ends.

The Homeless Storyline

Mr. Greg asks for the children's attention. He calls for last night's homework and begins to explain the math problem that would become today's homework assignment. He is interrupted by a knock on the portable door. The counselor comes into the classroom and behind her stands a small boy of Asian descent, shyly peeking around her, looking at the class and the teacher. Mr. Greg looks at the little boy, smiles, walks over and introduces himself. The counselor gives Mr. Greg some slips of paper, tells him, in a voice all can hear, that the child's name is Le and that "he is a bilingual."

This classroom reflects many aspects of our complex society, with its diverse population and cultures. Mr. Greg is attentive to opportunities that help his students become aware of the democratic principles to practice among themselves and in public. These principles are practiced within the community of the classroom, where a sense of belonging is fostered through trust, communal ways of understanding, and the feeling heart of compassionate imagination. With this new student, Mr. Greg seizes the opening to remind students of fairness and responsibility by engaging their compassionate imagination about one of the scariest, yet most common, of circumstances for school children: being the new student in a class. A stranger at the door, Le will be a part of the Storyline, working with the other children while at the same time adjusting to his new surroundings. Since the Storyline revolves around the implicit question of how do we treat strangers, this little boy provides Mr. Greg with a chance to help his students imagine other ways, besides exclusion, to bring him into the classroom.

Mr. Greg looks at the faces of his third grade class, who, in turn, are all eyes on Le. "Remember back to your first day of school?" he asks the class. "Who remembers what it is like to be at a new school?"

The children all raise their hands at once. He has got their attention. Everyone, it seems, remembers being "new." Mr. Greg is rapidly calling on each one and writing down their responses on the board: shy, nervous, scared, "Oh, don't leave me here." The board is full of their descriptions. "Do you remember what someone did to make you feel at home? What kinds of things did people do that made you feel better?" Mr. Greg queries.

This time the children take a few seconds to mull over their past experiences. Memories come to mind and hands go up again with such comments as "nothing," "they wanted to be friends," and "they were kind." But Mr. Greg isn't finished. He goes over to the corner where there is a large cage. Opening the door, he reaches in and pulls out Big Time, a huge, furry bunny, cuddling it in his arms.

Le has been seated in the empty desk and is mesmerized by the white furball. Mr. Greg has been told Le speaks Minh, but doesn't know if Le understands anything that is being said. But he has Le's attention. He stands near Le, holding Big Time and scratching the contented bunny behind the ears.

"I don't know if I told you my bus story," he says. The class chime in that they don't remember, so he has to tell it. Mr. Greg relates about his first day as a kindergartner on the bus. He was OK going to school, but on the way home, he didn't know where to get off so he rode the bus to the end of the line. The bus driver saw this little six year old and told him he had to get off, it was the end of the route. Luckily, another six year old was disembarking, too, and took the little boy home with him. Mother called mother and the boy was finally rescued. "But," said the teacher, "I was so scared." Murmurs of sympathy went through the room. The children knew what it was like to be so unsure.

Mr. Greg then asks for volunteers to make Le feel welcome and appoints two students who have raised their hands. However, so many hands are raised that he invites others who also want to welcome Le to feel free to do so. One of the third graders moves his chair over next to Le and smiles. Le smiles back and says, "Hi."

"What country did your folks come from?" asks Mr. Greg, as he pulls down the world map for all the children to see, not really sure if Le could understand his question.

"Alabama," says Le.

Without missing a beat, Mr. Greg goes over to the map and tries to locate the state on the big world map, gives up because the states are too small to see, and pulls down a large political map of the United States, asking a child to point out where Alabama is. Le smiles as another boy pulls his chair over to sit next to him.

The atmosphere of the room is calm and attentive. Mr. Greg makes a decision not to continue with the math lesson, which he finishes later in the day. Le is settling in and Mr. Greg wants to make sure he can participate if at all possible. And the rest of the class seems receptive right now. So Mr. Greg begins with the Storyline question. Mr. Greg looks at the children, who are sitting at their desks, looking back at him. He asks them, as if he is thinking out loud to himself. "What words come to mind when I say "homeless"?"

Children's own ideas and prior experience provide the starting point for the topic. Mr. Greg's question is the start of a Storyline, which begins with a conceptual question that marks the start of any Storyline—a question emphasizing the importance of encouraging the children to share their own conceptual model first. The conceptual question sets the stage for creating characters, when children will make their conceptual models of homeless characters.

A flurry of hands go up. As Mr. Greg calls out each name, he writes the child's answer on a large sheet of paper. This list will remain in view during the weeks when Storyline is going on, with children adding to it or using the words in their writing. The children gave these responses:

"It means without a home."
"It means to sleep in a shelter."
"No food or money."
"You sleep in alleys, subways, parks, and benches."
"It can mean you stay in a hotel."
"Maybe they have problems like drugs or alcohol."
"It means a hard life."
"They have to deal with others on the street."

The children's responses give no clue to their past behaviors and attitudes toward homeless persons. My presence, a new addition, could account for the "correctness" of their responses, which one might interpret as understanding and even empathy toward the plight of the homeless. However, I have taught and seen enough Storylines to know that such neutral or "correct" responses are common if the topic is uncomfortable for students—sometimes children share what they think the teacher wants to hear. Such responses might convince some teachers (or parents) that these children do understand about the unfortunate circumstances of those who are homeless, but the consistent behavior of the children belies a sense of compassion or empathy. Right answers do not necessarily reflect habits of mind.

As responses begin to repeat themselves, Mr. Greg asks another question. "Well," he says, "why are people homeless, do you think?"

More hands rise up and Mr. Greg calls on the students, writing their answers on another sheet of butcher paper.

> "They could have lost all their money."
> "Maybe they left their homes or ran away."
> "They could have been raised on the street."
> "And their house could have burned down."

There is a stir of discussion on this last comment. A year before, in the vicinity of the school, a string of arson fires had plagued the neighborhood. A majority of the children remember the fires and many know a victim, or at least know of a burned house in the neighborhood. During this discussion, one boy expresses fear his house would burn down. Another child agrees how scary that would be. And one boy volunteers that his family moved out of their apartment one day before the building caught fire and left all the tenants homeless. This is frighteningly real to him and to other children—to be burnt out of one's home with no place to go is terrifying. *When well done, Storyline creates a safe place where the children may take their fears and make them public often through their characters and the narrative, yet at the same time not draw attention directly to themselves, providing a safe space with distance to begin to think about the consequences of both their beliefs and behaviors.*

"He could have lost his job," says a child, turning back to the original question.

This comment gives Mr. Greg a chance to explain, "If one does not have a job, usually it means you have no insurance. Then, if you get sick, you cannot pay for health care." Mr. Greg follows up with an explanation whenever he is given an opportunity by a child's comment. In this case, he wants to make sure to bring out the connection between having a job and having health insurance.

"You can get homeless if you sell all your belongings; then you have nothing left," says a girl.

Mr. Greg then asks the children to break into pairs: "We are going to make a homeless character's face."

A mild form of pandemonium reigns for a few seconds as the children begin choosing partners. A protest starts up when Mr. Greg states, "Wait a minute. I am not finished. You have to find someone with whom you have not worked before."

"What?" goes the chorus of children's voices, but they leave off the protest in search of new partners. Wes says he would work with Le. Other children quickly find someone. Just in case someone is left out, Mr. Greg goes over to the piano and says over the din, "Lost and Found is over here. If you don't have a partner, come over here and we'll find you someone." But he is too late. Everyone seems to be paired off, and they've begun negotiating whose desk they would use to work together, though I notice two boys who seem to be working side by side, instead of together.

Mr. Greg reminds the children of the last time they had made a character in the astronaut Storyline done in the fall. He points at the construction paper and pens and scissors and glue he has set up on the side tables. *Preparation for a Storyline involves gathering a multitude of art supplies, so that all children can choose from an adequate array of materials: colored construction paper, pens, yarn, threads, glitter, wool, and remnants of fabric, and the like.* In anticipation of Mr. Greg and I beginning our Storyline, I had brought People Paper with me, flesh-toned construction paper in eighty shades, light to very dark skin colors. I notice how carefully each pair of children goes about deciding on the color of their character. Some pairs of children choose very light-colored paper for their character; others rummage around to find browns, both light and dark, to represent their character.

As I watch, the children create homeless people according to their ideas, experiences, and assumptions. As each pair of students works out details, I watch intently for how they come to make decisions about their character. One detail that takes a special amount of care are the eyes. Two children practice drawing eyes all over their desk. The desktop begins to be filled with bodiless gazes as the partners discuss the shape, the color, and the affect of the eyes they want for their character.

"I don't know how to make eyes," says Nino, who has been using his pencil to sketch out eye shapes on his desk.

"I don't know how to make *sad* eyes," says Juanita, his partner, who has been sketching eye shapes that covered every inch of her desktop.

"I like those!" says Nino, pointing to two eyes Juanita has just drawn.

"I like the way you drew that," he says, putting his finger on an eye. Juanita beams.

"What would he be looking at?" she asks.

"He would be looking at his friends," Nino replies.

This is different from art lessons often taught to schoolchildren, where a teacher draws a figure and asks children to practice copying it. Education is learning to ask questions. Where does that go? How can I make this face look like a face? This approach takes longer in the classroom, but once teachers get used to it, it gives more satisfaction. They don't want to go back to textbooks. In a Storyline, art is set within a context that fosters a need to know for the young artists. The ambiguity art affords gives rise to questions and different responses from the children about how they see the world. Here they experiment with just the right mood for their character's eyes.

When a teacher stimulates children's need to know about a topic or a skill, it can serve to sustain a sense of belonging, a sense of participation, a sense of community because the need to know comes from within the children, not imposed from without by the teacher. Even though it is the teacher who has set up and guides the Storyline through conceptual questions it is the children who navigate through their narrative and create the setting and characters.

The bell rings, interrupting the work in the room. It is time for recess. The students have been working on their characters for thirty minutes with deep concentration, and some want to stay in and continue.

"No. All of you go out for some fresh air," Mr. Greg says as he opens the door to a clear, almost sunny morning. The rain had stopped during the time the children were working.

I watch the children go out to recess. The playground is down the stairs, across a green strip of grass, and then down cement steps from the portable. Kim has an escort, as one of her classmates has her turn to lead Kim down the steps and see to it Kim comes back on time. She and the group of children surrounding her seem comfortable and easy, as they give her verbal descriptions of the path, the grassy patches, and the cement stairs leading to the play area.

Because Kim is one of the last to get to the swings and jungle gym equipment, it could be that she would rarely get her turn. Yet, children make room in line for Kim because they know she really likes swinging back and forth on the bars. The children know Kim; she is one of them, and their attitude is both respectful and accepting.

When the children come back to the room, Mr. Greg announces that we will begin introductions of the characters in five minutes. He asks that the children put their character on the blackboard if they are almost finished, so he can tell who is ready to introduce their character to the class. About ten characters plus two cats get taped to the blackboard. *It should be noted that while Storyline characters are usually placed in a setting represented by a mural or frieze, also created by the children, these characters will have no frieze because they are homeless. They take any space they can on the blackboard.*

Characters are a visual text created by the children. The characters the children create in a Storyline give teachers insight into their beliefs and concepts about a topic and about life. The context of a Storyline, in this case homelessness, provides many opportunities for the children to use all their senses, both in the exploration of their environment and in expressing their ideas about what they discover.

I am reminded how often children themselves feel homeless in school, as if there is no place for them. This Storyline has the potential to reveal how children might feel about school, as well as how they perceive the world, especially for the homeless, but also for themselves.

Brian Robbins is introduced to the class by his creators, Chase and Jason:

> Brian is 20 years old. He has been homeless since birth. His parents were living on the street. People helped Brian because he was young. They didn't help his parents because they were a little druggy looking. His parents were cold and hungry. They got sick and died.
>
> Brian lived with a family for one year. A family took him in and helped him. Then they found out he was doing drugs. They said he was a street person and that he wouldn't stop and they kicked him out.
>
> Brian went to private school for a while. It was a bad private school and they used to hit students with paddles if they did not follow the rules. He did not stay at school for very long.
>
> Brian loves to eat pizza. His favorite movie is *Hard Target*. He likes to listen to the Spin Doctors. He is sorry he could not see them when they were in Seattle, but the tickets were too expensive. He does not have any close friends, but he likes to play football. He usually plays football with other bums. Football is something that Brian does very well.
>
> Brian is afraid of guns and the police. He has stolen food, clothes (from the Bon Marche), and other things and he is afraid they might come after him.

I listen closely to Brian's story and catch the reference to "the other bums" that he plays football with. Such a comment contrasts with the children's list of opening notions given when Mr. Greg asked what it meant to be homeless. Then there were reasonable and sympathetic responses. Now as we see Brian and hear him, all of us in the audience are given another perspective, including one Chase and Jason may not intend to reveal. This gives the class and the teacher an opportunity to discuss issues when they are raised by such comments. I think Mr. Greg will wait to see if the children ask questions of Jason and Chase.

The children listen intently, and at the end of Brian Robbins's life story, they have no questions or comments. Then Wes and Le come up to introduce their character, Marcus:

> Marcus is fifteen years old. He has been homeless for around one year. He ran away from home because his mother and father beat him almost every day. They were both using drugs.
>
> Marcus does not have any close friends. He likes to eat soft tacos. He likes the music of Warren G. Marcus plays a lot of football, and he is very good at basketball.
>
> Marcus's favorite movie is *Street Fighter*. Marcus is afraid of the Grim Reaper. He is not sure of what that is, but he saw a picture of it and it scared him.

These children are conversant in pop culture. I note how much fast food they talk about, the music groups they like such as Spin Doctors and Warren G, and the movies they watch, for example, *Street Fighter*—all of this represented by their characters, of course.

Mr. Greg asks if anyone knows what the Grim Reaper is and no one does. "Well, the Grim Reaper is another word for death," said Mr. Greg, "and I would be afraid, too, just like Marcus."

During this introduction of Marcus, the class begins to ask questions of the character (and his creators Wes and Le). Students begin to feel personally involved in the creation of their character and in the Storyline they have produced. When children create an imaginary environment and inhabitants with whom they identify, they raise questions about areas they want clarified. *Storyline provides a forum for dealing with difficult or "extra" questions that usually are viewed as irrelevant or "off on a tangent" when the lessons are planned in advance and objectives are to be reached by the students.* When Marcus is described as liking the movie *Street Fighter*, a number of hands go up for questions.

"So how did Marcus get to see this movie without money?" asks Peter, who is always seeking to challenge anything and anyone who does not make sense to him.

Another student muses, "Maybe someone gave him a ticket."

This seemed to satisfy Peter who is trying to make sense of how Marcus could do things without money. Peter, I have noticed, sits in the middle of the room, but does not work with others. In fact, he is one of the boys I noticed who has decided to work alone on his character. In the days to follow, I see how often Peter is in conflict with his peers in the classroom and out on the playground. He seems to feel safe around Mr. Greg, who is very warm and accepting of Peter, yet who is always on the alert to set limits for him.

When Marcus is described as liking football, Mr. Greg asks if Marcus and Brian Robbins (who also likes to play football) ever play the game together. Wes ponders for a moment, then replies that he thought this was so, but he can't be sure.

The bell rings for lunch and the introductions come to a close as desks are cleared for sandwiches and milk. This morning time has seemed to fly by, both for me and for the children. *Storyline participants often remark how time slips away because of the intense engagement with an activity or discussion.*

Here in this room, Marcus, Brian Robbins, Dorothy, LizaLizard, and twelve more characters are born into the world of this class. They are not perfect people, but people who just are trying to live in the world. Their worries will emerge over the next few days as will their desires and dreams.

The next morning I walk into the portable and the children greet me with smiles and easy conversation that led to sharing about their characters. I wonder aloud how the partners had decided on names for their character. Because this is only the second day of the Storyline, the children will think over this question and let me know later, they say. But for now they show me that on the blackboard are nine new homeless characters, plus two pet cats. Mr. Greg comes over and tells me that characters are still being finished. He turns to the class.

"Let's get settled so we can work on our characters. Get with your partners so we can meet who is up there."

Mr. Greg points to the wall of Storyline characters, whose faces now peer out from their places on the blackboard. He takes seriously the work done by the students. These characters are part of this classroom, deserving of recognition, as are the other members. As characters interact with one another, as the children interact with the characters and each other, connections are formed that weave into the fabric of the community. This becomes a shared experience with characters, children, and teacher all interacting and participating.

"We met Brian and Marcus yesterday. In fact, we played a Spin Doctors compact disk at lunch just for Brian. Now let's finish working on our characters or their biographies." Today the children are writing a biography of their homeless character that must include how their character became homeless. *One of the purposes of Storyline is to provide children with opportunities to become familiar with the patterns of forms they will encounter as they grow up: applications for work, school, driver's license, or income tax. The pattern of name, address, phone number, and other pieces of vital statistics are part of the biography form the children write for their characters. After a number of Storylines, children begin to anticipate what they will need to think about in order to complete the biography sheet. The teacher can ask, for example, how old a character is, and what year he or she was born. For third graders, this becomes a computation practice as well as an exercise in making sense of other aspects of their characters' lives, such as how many siblings they have, or how old their parents are.*

Children pair up again (or in the case of Peter, work alone), cutting and coloring in the faces of their homeless character or discussing the aspects of their character's life for the biography. A blanket of low conversation hovers over the room as the children discuss questions about how their character became homeless or where he or she lives now or how old he or she is. Mr. Greg overhears one girl, Sue, tell how her homeless character, Chris, is "really good at sleeping."

"Oh, does he dream?" asks Mr. Greg.

Sue nods her head, "Yes, but he has scary dreams."

Wes joins in, "Then why does he like to sleep if he has scary dreams?"

"Different people worry him," she replies. "Chris is afraid they might hurt him. He finished school, but he has never worked at a job."

Peter, who is working at a nearby table, interjects. He had been listening to this exchange and kept shaking his head. "Well, he should go out and try. It doesn't cost anything to look for a job."

Sue tries to explain. "He thinks he can't find one because he is homeless and they won't like him." This satisfies Peter for the moment and both he and Sue turn back to writing about their character's life story.

The blind girl, Kim, and her partner, Dana, go up to the blackboard and say they are ready to introduce their character to everyone.

> Cortriy is 30 years old and has been homeless all of her life. Both her mother and father were homeless, born on the streets, too. Cortriy does not know where her

parents are now because she has not seen them for twenty years. They had had a big fight and that is when her parents left her. Maybe they're dead.

A voice from the other end of the room interjects, "Well, *that* was an unparent thing to do!"

"Man, cruel parents!" interjects another voice.

Well, Cortriy and her parents kept fighting about food. Her mother, father, and sister went away. They might still be together. But another sister accompanied Cortriy so she wouldn't be alone. She has a friend named Ralph.

"Oh," says Peter, "Are they married?"

"Ralph and Cortriy date," replies Kim.

"Are all three of them homeless?" asks Mr. Greg.

"Oh, yes. Cortriy and her sister Jennifer and Ralph are all homeless."

Cortriy loves pizza and taco salad. She has never heard music so she does not know what it is. And she has never seen a movie, either. No one will let her in to see one. She spends all her time looking for coins and money on the street, and for food. And she lives in the subway.

"When there is no food in garbage cans, what does Cortriy eat?" asks Sue.

Dana replies confidently, "Oh, she is very good at finding food in garbage cans. And she has no worries, never worries about anything." And with that remark, the girls go back to their seats.

"Let's hear from another character. Any volunteers?" asks Mr. Greg.

Sal and Bart, two boys, come up to the blackboard and take down their character, Robert, to introduce to the class.

Robert is 12 years old and has been homeless for two years. He got kicked out of his house because he couldn't pay his rent.

"You mean his whole family got kicked out?" asks Mr. Greg.

"No, because Robert wasn't living with his family. He was being abused by his whole family. Lots. That's why he ran away. He stole money. His parents died when he was ten. He is an only child."

"Where does he sleep?" asks Dana.

"Well, he sleeps in dumpsters. And he lives in an old subway," Bart responds.

"Then," asks Dana, "where does he go to the bathroom?"

"By a tree," both Sal and Bart say in unison. They had anticipated this question.

Sal and Bart have everyone's full attention and they continue Robert's story:

> Robert loves leftovers, like wishbones. His favorite music is Dr. Dret, but he doesn't have any favorite movies. Actually, he doesn't like movies. But he does like to find money in drainpipes and in the streets.

"Tell me," asks Mr. Greg. "What is the most amount of money Robert ever found at one time?"

"One dollar." replies Bart, with Sal nodding in agreement. "But he's real good at looking for food in dumpsters and garbage cans. He knows Cortriy, too, by sight. His fear is getting caught by the police."

Peter asks, "If the police actually arrest him, does he have a weapon to protect himself?"

"Yes," say the boys. "He has a metal fork."

"But why," asks Mr. Greg, "should Robert be afraid of the police at all?"

"Because of the way he looks," Bart says. "Robert looks scary even though he is not. He wears a yellow blanket and dreams when he sleeps. His dog died two days ago."

Here is one indication of imagination at work. Bart had participated in the rumors about the homeless in the park. Here, through his character, Robert, there is the idea that people can be afraid of someone because of their looks, even though they are not scary when you get to know them.

Sal takes up where Bart leaves off: "He dreams of a home, but he smokes because he wants to die." As Sal and Bart return to their seats, a number of children turn to their partners and mutter sympathetic sounds or criticism of Robert's wanting to die. The tone is subdued.

Mr. Greg gives this moment some space and time, allowing the children to absorb this new information about Robert. Mr. Greg does not rush to judge or make a value comment of any kind. Time is given for reflection about the moral issue of wanting to die.

Picking up on what Bart says about looks, Mr. Greg asks, "What kinds of words do we use to describe people? I mean any person, not just us or our characters."

Mr. Greg is asking another key question that guides children into thinking about how we see others. The words generated by the children are written on flip chart paper and are added to by the children as they think of additional words throughout the Storyline. The words are there for reference, to be used in their stories, their characters' journals, and in the verbal descriptions the children give about their characters. It is the children who create the details, though it is the teacher who asks the guiding questions. Also, when children's thoughts and words are written for all to see, and left up as a reference, the message is that their ideas are recognized as important. Even those children who may have a slow time writing, can see their contributions being recognized.

The underlying question Mr. Greg is driving at with this episode is "How much can you tell about people just by looking at them?" What may look good to one person does not to another. We are influenced more than we realize by the way a person looks, making assumptions that may not be accurate. Mr. Greg could tell the children this outright. Instead, he provides a way toward that thinking, if anyone is ready to do it.

A chorus of responses are written down on another flip chart sheet:

color of hair
feelings, happy or sad
look smart, or not
skin color
what they look like

Mr. Greg asks for examples:

well, dangerous or sweet

Now Mr. Greg turns our attention to the display of all our homeless characters, "So what words might we use to describe people? Any one of these characters, or all of them." Mr. Greg writes responses on the board:

electrified	weird	garbage diggers
ordinary	sad	green eyes
blue eyes	different	likable
dumped	sick	dirty

This new list has generated some words that reflect the attitude toward some of the people whom they teased in the park.

"What else do you notice about these people." Mr. Greg goes over to the wall where all the characters are posted. "I am curious. How many of our characters are there in all? How many men? women? Let's see. There are thirteen characters so far, nine men and four women, and we won't forget the two homeless cats Dorothy keeps as pets. So two out of every three are male." says Mr. Greg. "What do we have in terms of race? I mean like African American or Latino or White?"

Juanita and Nino raise their hands. Their character, Chris, speaks Spanish. Both Juanita and Nino were born in Spanish-speaking countries and are bilingual.

The children are turning to their partners to discuss race and language. So Mr. Greg asks if any of the homeless characters know each other. A number of interesting relationships are discovered as the children recount who knows whom.

"Karen and Christi know each other because they are sisters."

"Dorothy knows her cats, Hazel and Katie."

"TingTong and Redhead (characters whose makers are absent today but who have name tags under them to identify them)."

"What makes you think they know each other?" Mr. Greg asks, since the boys who created the characters are absent.

Sal answers right off, "Because they both look weird, that's why." *Appearances come up again and again. Listening to children and then posing questions to deepen or extend their understanding of a concept or belief allows for a teacher to foster links with the children's experience and critical inquiry. The climate of this classroom is consonant with the respect and recognition Mr. Greg wants to cultivate among his students. By being reflective and incorporating the students' discussion, there is a kind of collaboration between teacher and students that emerges, participative and interactive.*

This last question is an opening for Mr. Greg to guide the children to thinking about who likes or dislikes some characters. Again, this student is very confident that weirdness would be a reason to like one another.

"Hm, that is interesting," says Mr. Greg. "Then who might not like one another among our characters?"

Every hand in class shoots up as each child has an opinion. Everyone seems to know who does not like someone.

Mr. Greg calls on Sandra. "I don't think Karen and Jeff like each other because Jeff is not Karen's type!"

Peter can hardly contain himself, his arm is reaching to the ceiling and waving madly. Mr. Greg looks over at him and nods.

"TingTong and Cortriy definitely do not like one another because some blond hurt his best friend in the past and now he hates all blondes!!" (Cortriy has blond hair.)

Dana has had her hand up for a long time and Mr. Greg nods to her. "Well, Cortriy and Karen I know do *not* like each other because Cortriy thinks that Karen is *that* good and Cortriy doesn't like Christi because she is dirty."

Wes comments with total disgust, "They all hate each other!"

Socially, Wes knows what it feels like to be an outcast. School is not an easy place for him. Wes is a boy who reads very slowly and labors over writing. His spelling is still phonetic, and any word over two syllables presents difficulty either saying it or writing it. He is also one of the children who does not live in the neighborhood, being bused forty minutes each way to his home in the south end of town. But Wes finds a way to participate with his comments and additions to class discussions. He finds his words are written on the chart along with those of his classmates. His character is a part of the classroom community and has voice, just like the others.

Mr. Greg wonders aloud, "Hm, before you meet someone, do you have a sense if you'll like or not like that person? Can you tell? Or guess? What gives you the clues? How can you tell? Do you have any idea ahead of time?" As he muses to himself, the children become still and the mood reflective, with only two children whispering their opinions to one another. All the others are pensive. The mood has shifted.

Looking right at the class now, Mr. Greg asks, "Have you ever started liking someone, or not, and then the opposite feeling happened?"

Juanita can hardly contain herself, and her waving hand makes her the first to answer. "There was this girl once and I got to know her and she was nice, not mean."

"Well," prodded Mr. Greg, "how did you know she was nice?"

"I watched her," says Juanita. "One time no one else was around and I asked her if she wanted to play and she did."

Dana chimes in, "Yeah, but I have a friend who sometimes is really nice and sometimes is really mean."

"Oh," says Mr. Greg, "I'll bet we all know people we have hot and cold feelings about. Sometimes you really like them and then not."

Syd mumbles, "Sometimes a sister comes into my room and teases me and then *slams* the door."

Mr. Greg smiles sympathetically, "Ah, yes, siblings. Why don't we share with a partner a sibling story."

And this was exactly what they wanted to do. Snatches of stories filled the room as children told about experiences with their brothers and sisters. Mr. Greg could read the signs that the children were getting antsy. This was not the time to try to delve into disliking someone and then finding that you ended up liking them. Close to recess, Mr. Greg gives the children time to share their stories with one another.

When the bell rings, the children go out to recess still chatting about "the time when. . . ." I notice that Kim is being led out by another girl today, whose responsibility it is to look after Kim and help lead her back to class on time. "OK, can you find the door?" "Yes, of course I can," exclaims Kim "OK, now here is the porch. Step one, two, three. . . . Now we are going toward the playground." Kim begins counting the steps she is taking to herself. Mr. Greg told me that Kim wants to go to the playground on her own, and so she is counting each step. However, the playground is on the lower part of the school campus and only accessible by going down a flight of cement stairs. This is proving to be an obstacle for Kim, who still needs someone to let her know when she has arrived at the stairs to the playground. All the children in class are helping her whenever it is their turn to be Kim's guide.

The next day it is raining again. The children enter the portable when the first bell rings, shaking off their coats and hats, getting ready for class.

Mr. Greg tells them the principal is asking students to create a poster for Martin Luther King, Jr. Day later this month. All classrooms, even the primary ones, are invited to create posters in honor of MLK, while intermediate students are being encouraged to write essays.

Peter asks a bit indignantly, "Well, what if we want to do both?!" Peter is in a testy mood today. Mr. Greg knows when Peter is like this he really needs everything to be spelled out for him, boundaries, rules, expectations. This is partly why Peter finds it so difficult to work with the other children over a long period of time, and they have trouble working with him as well.

Dialogue between all participants in a classroom is a key principle of Storyline. Mr. Greg wants to extend the cooperative negotiation that occurs naturally in Storyline through dialogic interactions such as the one with Peter right now.

"Yes, you can write an essay if you want, but for third graders it is posters. But sure, any one of you who wants can write an essay and I am sure the principal will accept it," responds Mr. Greg.

Peter presses. "Well, what if we want to do *both?*"

Mr. Greg sees his question now and looks him right in the eye. "Yes, I see what you mean. Sure, go ahead if you want." Mr. Greg moves over to the blackboard where all the homeless characters are displayed.

"Now, we need to meet some characters. Jo, are you finished with yours? I see your partner isn't here today. Can we meet him, your character?"

Jo gets her character from the wall and quietly moves to the front of the classroom. Her shyness is evident, yet she seems comfortable addressing the group.

> This is King Kong and he is older than the universe, 12 × 9 years old.

"Where is he from?" queries Mr. Greg. "He can't be from Earth, because Earth is only five or six billion years old."

Jo is a very quiet student who also reads and writes slowly, which puts her behind in her classwork. She could be unsure of herself, but she has created a character who might fit in more easily in the earlier astronaut Storyline than in this one. But Mr. Greg's question shows he accepts King Kong. He has found that characters (or plots) from former Storylines sometimes creep into new ones.

Many students are shaking their heads. This does not make sense to them. One boy goes over to the bookshelf and pulls out a picture book of the universe as if to verify his doubts (or certainty) about King Kong's age. *A curious thing happens during a Storyline when someone says something that does not seem logical or sensible. When statements are made about a character, it is the creator's prerogative to explain reasons for their life history, their attitudes, and beliefs. And we who participate in a Storyline accept that what a creator says about the character is "truth," as only she or he really does know about the character in ways that the rest do not. The creator is the expert on the character. However, when a description like King Kong's is presented to us, billions of years old, it just makes no sense and we want to know how this came about.*

Our questions present challenges for the creator. What may have seemed like an interesting fantasy to Jo (who worked alone on King Kong because her partner was absent so much) now gives her a challenge to explain. So how will Jo posture King Kong who is "older than the universe" and integrate him into the story, I wondered.

> Well, King Kong is male and has been homeless 200 years!

Already some children are trying to figure this new piece of information out for themselves and turning to the south wall where astronaut characters from their Storyline last fall are still displayed. I overhear a couple of children explaining that King Kong could be one of the creatures Grandpa and Grandma Gladys (characters from the space Storyline) brought back with them.

"OK," says Mr. Greg, "How did King Kong become homeless?"

> The manager kicked him out of his house because he stopped paying the rent. He had to stop work which was creating toys. He is a toy maker.

Roger muses out loud, "Hey, maybe King Kong is at the New Universe Hotel."

Mr. Greg continues to encourage Jo, "Why did he stop working?"

> Oh, another company made newer toys and no one bought King Kong's toys anymore.

Jo seems satisfied with that answer, but still seems stuck. Mr. Greg asks another leading question. "What kind of toys were they then?"

> King Kong made alien toys.

Silence as Jo looks down at her feet.

"Well, can you tell us about his family?" Mr. Greg encouraged. Jo smiled and looked up.

> King Kong had a mother and a father and a dumb sister, but no one is living. They lived a long time, though. See, King Kong is not from this earth.

Silence again. Mr. Greg prods, "What kind of food does he like?"

> Oh, King Kong loves candy—any kind of candy. That's why he doesn't have any teeth!

Sure enough, Jo shows us King Kong's toothless smile—as she broadly smiles at us.

> He just loves movies about the homeless. He loves rap music from Da Brat. His favorite thing to do is to play kickball. He is best at playing kickball. He does worry about guns because he doesn't want to be shot. He has been shot at before. Any friends he had are all dead.

"Well, King Kong. Welcome to the world of the third grade homeless!" We exchange a glance that says we should move on to a critical episode. "So here is what we are going to do next. You will work with a partner. Today is the day that your homeless person becomes homeless. This is the day they left. And your task is to pack a bag to help them live on the street. What are some things you will need? You will probably think of more as you go along. We can add to our bag later on. Let's talk about what things you might need."

I move over to the board to write the children's responses as they are given. Again, we will keep this list up where everyone can refer to it, not only for ideas, but also for correct spellings of the words. Mr. Greg is handing out brown lunch bag size paper bags as I call on the children. They are already thinking, so the list is not as long as I thought it might become. It includes: bedding, toilets, food, toothbrush, soap, clothing, and a place to sleep. The children are already teamed up with their partner, intently trying to figure out what their character would need.

Juanita and Nino motion for me to join them. They are planning on what materials Chris will have as possessions. Gathering colored construction paper, scissors, glue, and marking pens, they prepare their list before beginning to fold and glue the items.

In a Storyline, the teacher plans well ahead to make sure she or he has a collection of mixed art materials and supplies all ready for the children. Many Storyline teachers collect odds and ends, from discarded notions and remnants at fabric stores, to raw, unprocessed wool from weavers, and the usual papers, magazines, pens, pencils, and crayons, and other art supplies. An important Storyline principle is that there be enough supplies and materials for everyone to choose from.

The transitions where children gather and choose their materials, move to work with their partners, and other collaborative work required within Storyline are noisy and purposeful. The noise is mostly from constant murmuring and from movement around the room as children find a space to set to their task of working and figuring out their plan for their character.

Juanita talks as much to her partner as to herself, "Chris will need a toothbrush and toothpaste. How about an apple? Yeah, he'll need an apple. Oh, and a sleeping bag, too. And a shirt and sweats." Juanita begins to draw the outline of a sweatshirt on blue construction paper. Before she cuts it out, however, I notice she is drawing a Bart Simpson face on the shirt she sketched.

While I am with Juanita and Nino, Mr. Greg is checking around the room to see if any one needs him. Henry, a boy sitting across from Nino asks, "Wait, how can I make the base to this glass?" The glass is construction paper, three dimensional cylinder, but without a base.

Dana volunteers to help him make the base because, "I can do that." Her offer of help is appreciated by Henry who thanks her and watches how she measures and cuts the paper.

This is a common occurrence in Storyline, where a need to know is brought up within a context. The child poses the problem, in this case about learning how to design a three-dimensional figure. There is room here for creativity, collaboration, and experimentation with what one knows and what one wants to know. Shared knowledge and skills are encouraged in Storyline.

Peter is off by himself, working solo on his character. With twenty-five students in the class, he opted to "stay single." Peter is cutting out a large green shape. Curious, I move over to his desk and ask him to tell me about this.

"This is Oscar from Sesame Street because Oscar IS homeless, don't you know? He lives in a garbage can and has flies all over him," he said, as he focused his attention back to cutting the green paper. Peter's character is interesting, because he is choosing something that already has a personality, and is known to most if not all the class. It is also Peter's way of not joining in, yet still being a part of the group.

When I move back to Nino and Juanita, they tell me they have just finished drawing a "portable toilet with realistic accessories." Their list is growing, and now they are drawing Chris's possessions all over a large piece of white construction paper. Chris owns quite a number of things that he drags with him in his bag. Nino and Juanita take turns showing me the drawings and telling me what each stands for. Nino points to their drawings as Juanita describes milk, sweatpants, pants, a sweatshirt, bread, gummy bears, apples and oranges, peanut butter, an empty bag, some coins, Cheetos and Ruffles chips, a sleeping bag, toothbrush, a TV, radio, boombox with compact disk player, pizza, apple pie slice, licorice, phone, a cup, and shoes, sox, and gloves. As they describe these items to me, they keep looking at each other with raised eyebrows when an item is named that may not be practical, such as a TV. There are some things to be figured out.

Conflict, both explicit and implicit, occurs throughout a Storyline, as children discuss dimensions of a character or frieze, accuracy of information about a word or a place, logic of a possession or contradictions within a character's biography. Conflict is expected, acknowledged, and used to help children learn to share their ideas in such a way that others can hear and understand. Here, conflict is not polarizing; it is, instead, the connecting glue of the classroom community during a Storyline. Negotiation is the norm, as are respect and civility. The anticipation of challenges produces thoughtful responses, even when the answer may be deferred, as in, "I'll have to check with my character later."

A tug on my shirt brings my attention to Bart, who wants to show us a paper plate he had created for Robert, his character. The materials are tinfoil, clay, and paper shaped to look like three dimensional representations of "pizza, raisins, Pepsi, cakes, and straws." All of this is covered with plastic wrap "from my lunch," Bart proclaims, proud of his ingenuity.

Bart is showing me the evidence of an episode from an afternoon session I could not attend. In that episode, Mr. Greg had asked the children to consider what a meal would be for their homeless character. Where would they get their food? How would they carry it around? When might they eat it? Mr. Greg uses Storyline throughout the day and week, sometimes scheduling another episode when it seems that the children either want to know or are ready to think about the question. Hence, over the two months of being in the class every morning and even some afternoons, I would still miss Storyline work Mr. Greg had his class do. I relied upon the children to tell me and explain what had transpired, usually by their description of a new artifact or piece of writing.

Because of its highly integrative nature, Storyline allows teachers the opportunity to address multiple teaching objectives in many different subject matters. Dramatic arts, in which the theater group led the students, gave rise to writing in their character's journal. Mr. Greg sets many objectives within this contextualized learning that develop a range of skills through critical curiosity and motivation that Storyline engenders in the participants. Curiosity is an important aspect of learning and is greatly encouraged by Mr. Greg, who is frequently heard throughout the day wondering about something someone did or said, or thinking "aloud" about a problem he has come across. His attitude is that problems are things we can figure out, sometimes alone, but also together. Habits of inquiry are formed by these small building blocks built into a Storyline. The search for answers to questions they have generated provides meaningful opportunities for the children to learn academic knowledge and to practice their skills of reading and writing, as well as negotiation and cooperation. Storyline is a powerfully social methodology because it promotes a range of values that are made explicit and public each time a character says or does anything.

"May I have your attention?" calls out Mr. Greg. "If when you are looking around the room and you see another person's idea—great! Share with other homeless characters. If you have a good idea for how to keep warm, for example, then share your idea."

In Storyline, children are encouraged to share their understanding and ideas of the world. Working together is encouraged because a Storyline principle is to be sure every single person in the class is involved and participating. However, the participation can take many forms, as we see with Jo and her King Kong character, and with Peter and Oscar. Sometimes children find it too difficult to create even a representation of something that may come too close to home for them. So they create a character who may participate in a parallel way with the other characters, keeping apart from but also a part of the group. Often when this occurs, if a teacher gives the children room to explore the topic and discover that it is safe to risk talking about what they think, then ideas and beliefs begin to be shared. This is done through their character and in their discussions as the class engages in making the story together, guided by the teacher's questions. Undergirding Storyline is the belief that children need to feel that they can trust before they reveal important matters. Trust develops over time and within the context of participation in a group.

Bart smiles, and goes off to another couple of children to show his handiwork. Hal, who had been sitting at a nearby table working with his partner, moves his chair over to where Nino and Juanita are. "Wait a minute," he chimes in, "your toilet has to be hooked up to running water. Where are you keeping your toilet?"

Juanita argues, "Chris will not need running water where he is in the alley. He can empty it whenever he uses it."

Time has passed so quickly this morning that when Mr. Greg asks people to start cleaning up to prepare for the theatre group which regularly comes in to lead the children in creative dramatics, it takes a few seconds to lift their interest out of their homeless character's possessions and back to class routine.

Use of drama is important to Mr. Greg. He has invited a theater group to come in weekly and lead the children in creative dramatics, and to give them a feel for the tools of an actor. This afternoon Mr. Greg will have the theater group lead the children in creative movement, such as different ways of walking. Ultimately, this will lead to another Storyline question: How does your character walk? Why does she or he walk this way? How does the way a person walks reveal who they are? Through such experiences, the children's imagination is developed as they try to think about who their character is and how she or he would move. When we begin to think about another person, especially one who we think is different than we are, and endow that person with meaning, we become a kind of participant observer in our imaginations. We must conjure up in our mind's eye how that person looks, walks, talks, feels. In this conjuring we encounter the person as someone less different. This is the promise of the arts, particularly where children are active participants.

Quietly, they carefully put the possessions away in a box or in their desk where they will be safe until they work on it again.

Next morning, the sun is out, the sky a clear blue with only a hint of a chilly wind coming from the north. As I walk up the pathway to the portable, Peter, Juanita, Nino, and Bart skip up to me, pronouncing Rosalia.

Only Juanita gets the soft roll of the first syllable. "Hi. I am so glad to see you."

"Does anyone know who will be introducing their character to us today?" Peter nods, then dashes up the steps into the classroom, perhaps to guarantee that he is called on today.

Peter leaves very little to chance, I have noticed. He prefers to work alone as often as he can get away with it, and will take out some of his internal frustration with others out on the play field. His keen sense of justice and fine intellect contribute to his insistence that rules be followed. Others like Bart and Henry try to include Peter in games, but it is usual to have Peter perceive others not following the rules and then he demands the game be stopped. Yelling matches frequently ensue, with Peter protesting loudly and indignantly to Mr. Greg, with whom he seems to have a sense of trust. But with his classmates, Peter keeps himself distanced with his sharp tongue.

As the class settles down at their desks, Mr. Greg asks for volunteers to introduce their character, with Peter shooting up his hand. Even as Mr. Greg nods, Peter is up at the front, holding Oscar, his homeless character:

> Nobody knows how old Oscar the Grouch is. He has been homeless all his life. His parents and sister have been homeless for all of their lives, too. They all live in garbage cans. They have never wanted to live anywhere else. Oscar's mom lives in California. His sister lives in Oregon. His four cousins live in Florida. They are gray instead of green. Oscar lives alone, but he does see his family sometimes.
>
> Oscar's favorite food is pizza with garbage on top. His favorite garbage is aluminum cans. He loves horror movies, and his favorite song is "On Top of the Schoolhouse."
>
> Oscar's best friend is Slimy the worm. Slimy can be pretty mean. Big Bird didn't like him and said he didn't want to be friends anymore. Oscar likes it when Slimy is mean and so they are good friends.
>
> Oscar really likes to put people down. He is very good at it and does it a lot. He also likes to write graffiti on things. He really likes to write graffiti about Big Bird. He does not like Big Bird at all.
>
> Oscar is angry about everything, but he is not afraid or worried about anything. He does not like garbage men very much. In fact, he would be real happy if there were no garbage men.

Peter's presentation catches my attention. Since he has a character, Oscar, from Sesame Street, he is defined by that character's personality, which everyone knows. Yet, he imbues Oscar with facets that others, including myself, had not realized. We knew, for example, that Oscar is angry about a lot of things, but I found it interesting Peter added that Oscar was not afraid or worried.

Peter is satisfied with his presentation and sits down without waiting for questions. Mr. Greg asks for the next presenter to please come up. Raymond is a boy who was here for the first couple of days of the Storyline, but has been absent over a week, which according to Mr. Greg is a common occurrence for Raymond. Though Raymond is a bright, gentle boy, his frequent long absences hinder his learning of skills and, moreover, interrupt his relationship with his classmates. He is usually far behind in all his work, which he does painstakingly slowly anyway. Mr. Greg mentioned that Raymond's home situation is a major cause of these absences, so when Raymond is in class, Mr. Greg makes sure that he participates and is made to feel part of the group. It is an important step for Raymond to come up to the front of the room, holding his character, Kurt, who has been known only as "Redhead" by the other children, so named for the bright red hood over his head. Everyone is curious about "Redhead." Since Raymond was gone for so long, everyone in class began calling his character Redhead, and all agreed that would be his name until Raymond came back to introduce Redhead to us all:

> Kurt is a man who has been homeless for a long time. His house burnt down. He was living with his mother and father, but he lost both parents in the fire. He had no brothers or sisters.

Mr. Greg and I make eye contact. We know that there was a tragic fire recently that had made the front pages of the newspaper, following the loss of lives of four firefighters. You couldn't turn on the TV without images of the blaze and accompanying news of the fire.

"Did Kurt have any insurance?" asked Mr. Greg.

> No, he just crawled around the street.

"*Wait* a minute," challenges Peter. "What did people do when they saw a baby?"

> No one paid any attention to him. And he ate leftovers from the streets. His favorite food is ramen. And his favorite movie is *Street Fighter.*

Peter challenges once more. "How did he see this movie if it just came out?"

This time, Raymond ignores Peter's question, and his voice is getting quieter.

> Kurt really likes Nirvana as his favorite music.

"What's Kurt best at doing?" asks Mr. Greg, trying to encourage Raymond into telling us more about his character's personality.

> Looking for food, that is what he is best at.

"Has Kurt ever worked? Has he ever earned money?" queried Mr. Greg.

Raymond looks straight at Peter when he answers.

> Kurt has helped garbage men. And he likes to look at the stars.
> [Raymond then tells us that he has a telescope at home that has lost a leg on its tripod.]

"Well, does he have any friends?" Mr. Greg asks.

> No, Kurt doesn't have any friends because he is homeless.

Is this a connection to the homeless people in the park? I wondered.

"Well, they wouldn't be real friends anyway," exclaims Peter.

This comment of Peter's does not surprise me. I have been watching him in class and out on the playground for about a month now and have observed him arguing passionately over rules or procedure with just about everyone in class, including Mr. Greg. Mr. Greg tries to anticipate these episodes, but often, he tells me, Peter just erupts. Then Mr. Greg attempts to help sort out the perceived offense and work through the problem with him. Making friends is not easy for Peter.

Raymond goes back to his seat saying there is nothing more to tell about Kurt. So Mr. Greg asks for the last two characters to be introduced, LizaLizard and Annie.

Syd and Grace are two vivacious girls who enjoy being the center of attention. No shyness here, only bright, eager faces, ready to introduce LizaLizard to the class.

> This is LizaLizard. She is 18 years old, and she has been homeless for two years. She ran away from her house. Both of her parents died. They caught cancer. She met Dorothy on the street.

"Dorothy and LizaLizard are friends? What kinds of things do they like to do?" asked Mr. Greg.

> They like to play tag and to read. In fact they really like to read *Wizard of Oz* books. Their favorite food is apples and oranges. And they like the movie *Lady and the Tramp*. Their favorite music is Beethoven.

Katie and Hazel are friends with Pooch and Tabby, Dorothy's and LizaLizard's stray pets of two dogs and two cats. Liza loves animals. She sleeps in an old doghouse with Pooch. She is afraid that her home will be torn down so that she has nowhere to stay. She and cousin Jennifer know each other. [Cousin Jennifer is another character from the astronaut Storyline].

Syd and Grace sit down. Then Le and two other children have to get up to leave for their special ESL (English as a second language) class, interrupting the presentation. This is a frequent occurrence in most schools, where interruptions are common as students are pulled out for special classes. Mr. Greg waits for them to leave, then says to the class, "I know you are working on your homeless bags, but can we have your attention for this character?" The children not-too-subtly slow down, not stop, working. They all look up at Sally and Tanya, who are about to introduce their character, Annie, to let them know they are listening and it better be interesting!

Annie is 15 years old. She has been homeless for about three years. There was a fire that burned down her house. Her mother and father were killed in the fire. Annie ran from the house. She was scared and crying. She went behind the garbage dump and stayed there.

Annie has friends, now. She met Dorothy and Liza. And she stays with her dog Boney and her cat Fluffy. She lives in an old dog house in the dump. She often stays with Liza.

Annie likes to eat fruit. Winnie the Pooh is the only movie she has ever seen. She used to own it before it burned in the fire. She watched it over and over. Annie likes the music of Los Lobos.

Annie is very good at reading, too. She can read so well that she knows the biggest word in the dictionary. She can read it, spell it, and say it.

She is worried, though, that the cops will find her and take her to jail. See, she stole some fruit from a wedding one day when she was hungry. Sometimes she is so hungry she stands on a street corner with a sign that says Feed Me. Annie is 90 lbs. and is about average height for a teenager.

She used to go to school, before the fire. She was an excellent student. She was a very good reader and was good at acting in plays. She could not go back after the fire. She did not want anyone to know she was homeless. Annie had a boyfriend named Mark, but she never talked to him again after the fire. He did not know where she was. She had two close friends at school, Syd and Grace. She has not seen them, either.

"Well, now we have all our characters introduced of all who are here. Let's see how much we can remember of who is up here on the board." The children call out each character by name and offer some critical attribute they recall. Our homeless characters make an interesting group, each with distinctive personalities and features. The recess bell rings and as the children leave to go out, I notice that they are listing other features of the characters on their way to the playground.

Next time the children will be reading the stories they wrote about their characters and sharing their bag of possessions with us. So far they have been writing biographies and introducing them in front of the class. Characters are known and their stories remembered, so creating context is given a more complex twist. The children expect to be challenged if something they describe does not make sense with what they have said before.

The children are back from recess, ready to work. Mr. Greg asks them to take out their homeless folder, which now has all of their characters' biographies the children created, but Mr. Greg has typed each one out, along with the author's name at the bottom of each character's life history. Reading these aloud, each pair will take a turn, and from the looks of it they all are eager to read to one another the text they have produced.

Mr. Greg types each child's journal entries at the end of every day of writing so that the next day he can hand out the typed three-hole punched pages for them to put into their folders. The folders are punched and clips put into the holes to secure the papers, making it easy to add or take out as needed. The children feel the power of both their authorship and authority in the written word. And the children listen carefully, as they read silently along with the author.

The children raise their hands to read aloud. Juanita is called upon, and she and Nino take turns reading about Chris. Juanita is not a strong reader, yet her voice is clear and confident as she reads the words she and Nino composed. She reads her story. Faltering over some words, Juanita perkily reads, stumbles, gets prompted by other students, figures out the word, then continues. She gets through her half slowly and with an air of accomplishment, and Nino takes over. Nino is a fluent reader, and finishes reciting his half in a couple of minutes. Both Juanita and Nino beam as they read their words. The other children are all listening attentively, knowing they will be called on to do the same. Throughout the week Mr. Greg has given the children this reading lesson, where one or two pairs read their own words about their character outloud to the class. This reading lesson also brings everyone up to date by reviewing each character. It is as if the children are hearing about these characters for the first time, they pay such close attention.

Perhaps it is because their stories are written by them, but there is a serious mood when someone is reading from their homeless folder. Since each character's story is in every folder, the children can follow along as the author reads aloud. Even a slow reader finds sanctuary in the written word. And I am also struck by the absence of questions or challenge during a reading. Even Peter is respectful and patient throughout. Everyone is an author in print.

Mr. Greg picks up on the mood and says, "We've now met and read about all our homeless characters. Let's start looking at what people have packed in their bags. I want to go over ideas about this. If someone has something in their bag and you want to add it to your stuff, write the item on the outside of your paper bag to remind you to make it later. If you have any questions about why someone has included something in the bag, then ask him or her about it." He turns to Mary and Rita and asks, "What is Dorothy bringing with her?"

Dorothy is a character of these two girls, who love the Baum series about Oz. Dorothy is a character from *The Wizard of Oz*, who is also homeless, made so by a tornado. This Dorothy (whose last name is the same as the Dorothy in Baum's book, Gale) is also able to make her way in the world. There is a positive attitude and resourcefulness about her.

Mary and Rita pull out Dorothy's things to show us. From out of the brown bag comes a *Wizard of Oz* book, a study book to write stories in, grapes, carrots, apples, and three pears, toys for Katie, Hazel, and ToTo to play with, a jug of water, and a bone.

Hands shoot to the air when they hear this last item. "What kind of bone?" "Yeah, which animal is gonna use the bone?"

Mary patiently explains the bone is for Dorothy's cats.

This is too much for Peter. "Cats?!" Cats don't eat bones. Dontcha have any cat food?"

Rita and Mary look at each other confidently and assure Peter that they will find some cat food for their cats. They sit down and Bart and Sal take their places to talk about their character, Robert.

"Here's Robert's list of things. Shirt. Wallet. Shoes. A black heart. A plate of food. Weapon. Store keys for Toys R Us. Change. Basketball (Robert loovvves basketball). A throw up bag. A plate of food."

Bart chimes in, "Robert is a vegetarian. Here is what is on his plate. He's got Pepsi, pizza, cake, rice cakes, corn, and green beans."

Juanita asks, "Why does Robert have a black heart?"

Bart and Sal shake their heads. They can't recall why this is on their list. But the real issue is about that weapon. When asked why Robert has to carry a weapon at all, Bart replies, "He hits cops with it and steals their wallets, that's how he gets his money." This answer sparks discussion among the children, leaving Bart and Sal standing in front, listening.

Questions they can hear their peers discuss is whether it is practical to carry a weapon. Another student thinks aloud, "What if someone finds it on him and then uses it against him?" and "What if he can't keep it hidden and someone sees it?" and "What if he plays basketball and can't leave the weapon in his bag? What's he gonna do with it?"

Mr. Greg is watching the boys as they listen to all this dialogue. He says to them, "It's a question of whether he can keep doing this—both keeping the weapon and assaulting police officers."

Bart tries to save some dignity for Robert by pulling out of the bag an album of family portraits. "See, here is Robert's photo album of his family and his brothers and sisters so he doesn't forget them." Only one student comments, and that a bit sardonically, "Yeah, nice family photos."

Ron gets up to show us Jeff's possessions. Ron decided he wanted to work alone on his character, and has been keeping to himself, not sharing anecdotes or comments as the others do about their characters. So we all know that Jeff is also a loner and not very social.

Ron begins to list out Jeff's possessions. "He's got a knife, some cigarettes, gloves to keep his hands warm, soda pop, boombox, and some hand grenades."

Juanita does a dramatic double-take at Ron and says, "What kind of a person is he that he needs all these weapons?"

Nino spouts, "Hey, doesn't he know how dangerous it is to carry hand grenades? He could blow people up, maybe even himself."

Peter cannot contain himself, "OK, so he's got weapons. But where's his food? Doesn't the guy need to eat?"

Ron does not seem to have thought of that so makes up an explanation for us. "Well, Jeff keeps his weapons hidden so people don't see them. But he uses them to rob people and get food."

Mr. Greg interjects, "But when you stab someone, or rob them, you get in serious trouble, right?"

"Yeah," says Ron, "so Jeff never gets caught. He's got a knife, a gun, and two hand grenades." (The weapons have now increased to include a gun.)

Mr. Greg persists, "I'm afraid he'll be real dangerous."

Chase is scowling, ". . . a grenade is so powerful." This arsenal has incensed some children, puzzled others, and hands are waving to be called on to ask a question of Ron.

"Has Jeff ever been attacked?" asks Dana.

"Isn't he a little bit scary to other people?" ponders Chase.

"I wonder if Jeff has any friends or are they all too afraid of him?" I ask Ron.

Ron mediates his answer to all of us, "Jeff keeps all his weapons deep in his pocket or bag so nobody can see them."

But Chase won't let this go by. "But what if he forgets?"

Ron looks indignant, "Well, he's not stupid, you know!"

"Yeah," retorts Chase, "but he doesn't go to school, though."

Shaking his head, Peter interrupts, "You don't have to go to school to learn. You can learn lots without going to school. . . ."

Mr. Greg says, "We've met some characters: Jeff and Robert, who have weapons with them. Sounds like being on the street is not so simple and there is lots of potential for violence. You have to watch out for violence. What kinds of dangers do homeless people face, I wonder?"

The class has become very quiet. Without raising her hand, Sue says softly, "Some people are afraid of the homeless, so they threaten them."

Sue's comment ripples across the room in silence. Are the children thinking about the times they teased or listened enthusiastically to another student's teasing of a homeless person? Mr. Greg lets the moment hang in the air.

Our reflection is broken by the voice of the librarian on the intercom, announcing that the library was now open for us. Mr. Greg asks the children to line up, and to not forget their homework assignment—have their character "write" seven sentences in their homeless journal—and he will read them aloud, a few a day for the rest of the week.

Next morning, there is a sober atmosphere in class. Mr. Greg begins by reading a journal entry about what happened to Chris. As he reads aloud, the children are all eyes on him, listening very hard.

"Last night I slept in the alley. In the morning I woke up and looked for breakfast. I looked behind a restaurant for food. In the dumpster I found part of a cheeseburger. I ate it."

The children remain still. Mr. Greg reads a few more journals out loud. Then he goes over to the blackboard, asking the children write the following on the side of a piece of paper that will go in their homeless folder:

I SEE. . . .
I HEAR. . . .
I SMELL. . . .
I TOUCH. . . .
I TASTE. . . .
I FEEL. . . .

"Now write what your character saw, heard, smelled, touched, tasted, and felt sometime yesterday, maybe when he or she woke up. Let's write that now." The children are imagining, thinking, and writing their Sense Poem. Here are two examples:

I see an alley
I hear cars
I smell dirt
I touch the hard ground
I taste nothing
I feel sad.

I see the morning sun
I hear birds singing
I smell the earth
I touch the wet grass
I taste the water
I feel awake.

The children share their poems with one another and place them carefully in their homeless folder, growing thicker with their writing typed out each night by Mr. Greg. Mr. Greg goes to the front of the room and asks, "What have you heard about Japan's earthquake?" Kobe, Japan, has been hit by a major earthquake that has leveled the city, leaving thousands dead and hundreds of thousands without homes. The children are alert and call out answers.

"Scary." "Some people were sleeping when it happened." "A hospital got knocked over and patients died."

"Wait," says Wes, "I have a question. How do earthquakes happen?"

Rita muses, "I heard the ground rubs up against itself."

Sean nods, "It has something to do with mountains."

Dana recalls, "My grandmother felt an earthquake once."

Mr. Greg gets the globe. "Let me tell you something about how earthquakes happen. . . . Look at the globe. It shows land and water. Everything sits on plates." Mr. Greg retrieves a tin plate from the bunny cage. "There are twelve plates on earth." He grabs the attendance envelope. "This is the United States. It sits on a plate and the plate is constantly moving very slowly."

Rita exclaims, "Yeah! That's what I meant!"

"OK," continues Mr. Greg. "Put your fists together and push. One goes up and one fist goes down."

"A handquake!" quips someone.

Mr. Greg now turns the globe, saying the name of the plate as he turns it: "Eurasian plate, Pacific Ocean plate, Philippine plate . . . ."

"Hey," interjects Kim, "that's where I'm from!" But the rest of the class is listening with rapt attention. No one is talking. They wait for Mr. Greg to continue. They all want to know how earthquakes occur.

"So, if you push hard enough, like with your fists, you shake and move even mountains."

"Oh," says Peter aloud, "it's like Atlantis, that island that sank because of an earthquake, and now it's lost and nobody can find it. But they know it existed."

Wes is worried. "Do we have a plate?"

"Yes," says Mr. Greg, "we are on plates, too. Los Angeles, San Francisco, Seattle."

"When I was in California once, I felt a small earthquake," Peter shares.

Sean wants to know what happens in a small earthquake.

Wes now shares why he seems worried. "My grandmother was in an earthquake here in Seattle. Her house shook, and only part of her upstairs came down."

Chase shares that his mother has also felt an earthquake.

We are looking at how a teacher can use a current event and turn it into a science lesson because the children have a desire to know what an earthquake is. The informality of this classroom is deceiving; serious work goes on here within an ethos of civility and trust. For Wes to ask in front of his classmates and for Mr. Greg to explain what an earthquake was is evidence of that trust. Mr. Greg takes it further, by connecting the earthquake victims with homeless people.

"What do you think of the people in Kobe, Japan? They aren't drug addicts or without jobs, but they are now homeless. What don't they have now that they need, do you suppose?"

Instantly all hands are raised, and Mr. Greg writes on the board as ideas are called out. "They don't have enough food." "No home or shelter." "They need water that's clean." "Yeah, and bedding to sleep in." "They don't have any shops to get stuff." "I bet they don't have enough clothes." "I know. They need a hospital." "Or maybe they just need a place to go for medicine and help." "What if they lost their eyeglasses and couldn't see?" "Hey, they might not have any electricity."

"What couldn't you do if there was no electricity?" ponders Mr. Greg.

Heads are shaking. "No TV." "No radio." "You'd have trouble reaching 911." "No heater." "Your food will go rotten." "You couldn't call your family or friends." "No lights and no blow dryer."

Mr. Greg nods his head. "Maybe we should listen to the radio and read the newspaper to see what is happening to the people over in Kobe. We'll be talking about this some more as we hear about what the people need." Again we have discussed this until the bell heralds that it is lunchtime.

Mr. Greg and I want the children to finish sharing what their characters took with them in their bags, and a couple children who have been absent still need to finish. So I sit down next to Wes, who is Marcus's creator, and someone whose reading and writing skills are not very strong. Wes and I have worked together before so I feel comfortable just sitting near him.

"Maybe those of you who haven't had time can just jot down items on your paper bag. Sit with your partners if you want and write down ideas." This is in lieu of actually creating the item out of construction paper and then placing it in their bag.

Wes looks at me and asks if I would please help him write down his list for Marcus. We work closely for ten intense minutes on his list of twenty-four items Marcus will be taking with him. Wes tells me what to write on the bag, and I do it. As I print out each item, he thinks aloud, and regularly checks with me to see that I put down an item. I show him the word for the item, and then he says, "Yeah, Marcus had that." A rhythm develops as we quietly work together.

Class begins again and Mr. Greg calls for someone to present their homeless bags. Wes raises his hand, but he is too slow. Chase gets called on to tell what Brian Robbins took with him. Wes listens carefully to the list of items, but he also practices reading the printed list I wrote for him on his bag, whispering to me for confirmation if he is unsure what a word is. Then he whispers the word to himself, going through his list methodically. When Chase sits down, Wes immediately waves his hand to be next.

Mr. Greg calls on Wes next, and he double checks with me one more word before standing up by his desk and giving Marcus's list.

water	pizza	Sweat suit	shorts
clippers for his hair	batteries	pajamas	apple
football	shirt	coat	bus transfer
pants	glasses	shoes	socks & underwear
a cellular phone that he found thrown away	and a place to stay.	toothbrush/ paste	hat
necklace & ring			
$10 from his job			

"What??!" Peter and Juanita protest this last item. "What does *this* mean? How can you carry a place to stay?" This does not make sense to a number of the other children either, and they discuss aloud what Marcus is doing with a place. Mr. Greg uses the children's discussion to scaffold to another level. He chimes in, "Think about how Marcus takes care of his stuff. So no one takes it. He has a lot of things, doesn't he?"

Wes confidently addresses both the students and Mr. Greg, "He *doesn't* carry it around. He's living in an old abandoned house."

"Then how can he be homeless?" retorts Peter. This prompts some children to briefly discuss the idea of being homeless with a place to go to. Mr. Greg interrupts and reminds everyone that this place is supposed to be abandoned.

Wes reminds us, "It's not a house Marcus owns, only that no one is living there and he sleeps there and stores some of his things there."

Mr. Greg is always alert for an appropriate opening to reinforce or develop the children's thinking about a topic. Wes has just given him this opportunity to focus the students on how the homeless must necessarily struggle with what most of us take for granted: a place to keep things. Through the use of student ideas and comments, he can extend the students' conceptual notions of the homeless through his own questions.

Mr. Greg looks around the room. "Each of your characters has a bag he or she is carrying around things in. Large bags are not the best way to carry your things. Can you design a carrying set up so that the homeless can carry their things around the city? What are the things you have to be concerned with?"

"Security." "Weatherproof," "Not too big."

Another bell interrupts our discussion, and I leave for a class I teach at the university. I know that by tomorrow bags will have been designed to protect characters' possessions.

The next day is Friday and when I arrive, a large collection of cans, blankets, and other staples is in the corner. The children got the idea to organize a drive to help the people of Kobe. Mr. Greg had called the Japanese Consulate and was told there would be a drop-off place for items to be shipped by plane to Kobe. Any class that is interested has been invited to bring in items suggested by the Consulate.

Storyline provides myriad chances to the teacher to connect to what is happening in the world with the children's experience. Mr. Greg used the opportunity this Storyline offered to link the Kobe earthquake with the plight of the homeless in the park. The compassionate imagination that the stories from Kobe arouse in the children's minds makes a short leap for them to think about their own homeless character with a feeling heart. How much further is it for them to go now to consider those in the park, the streets, the alleys?

The children are getting ready to listen to a classmate discuss his carry-all. Peter raises his hand, then quickly puts it down and shakes his head. Too late. Mr. Greg calls on him. Peter shuffles to the front of the room carrying other rumpled paper bags. Out of one he begins pulling out little characters!

> These are Oscar's friends. Here is Brainy. Helps Oscar do practical jokes 'cause his brain is alive. This is mean Rainbow Noisy (a relative of Mr. Noisy). Oh, here is a canoe (shows miniature canoe he cut out from construction paper) for little guys who get caught in puddles. And Stick Man. He kinda messes things up sometimes. And Strikeman, Big Bird's friend who always goes on strike and teams up with Oscar instead. All these guys help Oscar fight.

Here in this little bag are the facets of Peter himself, in all sorts of fragmented characters. These little characters reflect Peter in many ways: the emphasis on brains, joking, messing up, and fighting.

Turning to his other brown bag, Peter catalogs all of Oscar's things.

> "Gum to mess up his hair with." "Rotten bananas." "Oscar's flag."
>
> "Cigars ('cause they smell bad!)." "Butterfinger, all melted and stale."
>
> "And Oscar's place stinks like heck! He lives in a garbage can and he loves garbage." "His favorite drawing: Dead Big Bird." "Rotten apples."
>
> "Super Peanut." "Bony fish."
>
> "Oops, here's Invisible Man in the wrong bag. Must be 'cause you can see right through him!"

As other children take their turn I let my thoughts turn to Peter, who on the first day of my visits to his classroom, kept a sharp eye on me throughout the entire morning until recess. I would be gazing around the room, and just catch Peter lowering his eyes in case I saw him looking at me. He worked alone by choice, but after watching his interactions with other students around him, I think it is not easy for him to collaborate with others. His opinions, along with a testy, belligerent manner, keep others at arm's length from him. However, Peter has a role to play in this class. He is a critical observer, rather than an outright participant. I note that Peter can be counted on to ask a question with a moral slant or one based on trying to make sense of something; for instance, he will question a character's story that may have contradictions. Such conflicts annoy him, and Mr. Greg is sensitive to Peter's short fuse, which he defuses with looks or a hand on his shoulder or an inclining ear.

I am interested in Peter's sharing of his extra bag full of characters—multiple characters who all live with Oscar in his garbage can. Each character seems to represent some part of the real Peter who does indeed protest loudly, especially on the playground, that other students might "go on strike" and team up against him. Or Stick Man, who "kinda messes things up." And I am struck by how Peter emphasizes intelligence, who is and who isn't, in his conversations about all these characters.

Though Peter has gone along in the Storyline with creating a character, writing in his homeless journal, sharing his belongings, he has also kept to himself, too. He doesn't speak for Oscar or about Oscar very much, though when he does it is to make some point about Oscar, as in, "Of course he stinks! He LIVES in a garbage can!" However, during presentations by the other children, Peter can be counted on to ask direct, pertinent questions, such as, "How can he be homeless if he has a job?"

Back from a three-day weekend, Mr. Greg has asked the children to write seven sentences as "your homeless character, 'I' sentences." After a long weekend Mr. Greg says the class is hard to "get started." Using their homeless journals to write a few lines helps bring them back to school routine. Prompting those who were slow starting, Mr. Greg asks leading questions, "What did they do over the weekend? Please find a blank page in your homeless journal book and begin writing."

Peter begins writing in his homeless journal. *Katherine Paterson writes that the basic task of education is the stretching and nourishment of the imagination through myths, legends and stories, which are at the very heart of the process. Writing of this kind, which reinforces children's capacity to imagine how another feels or might act or lives out a weekend, is exactly the stretching that Paterson means. To see as with the eyes of another invites children to go inside of themselves and cross the bridge to imagine what the Other experiences.*[2] Other children follow suit and the sound of scraping pencils and sounding out words takes over the room as the children write in their journals, some looking up at the charts still hanging on the walls for spelling of words. Some children incorporate actual events from the weekend in what their character did. Chris, for example, was able to watch the Superbowl by watching the TV from a store that had one in its window.

"OK," says Mr. Greg. "Let's think some more about words. What kinds of words can you use to describe a place?"

"You could draw and then tell what you drew," responds Juanita.

"You could think of a thing and then describe it," says Raymond.

". . . so that someone else would be able to know exactly where you're talking about," Mr. Greg clarifies.

"Well, a bed, it could be in the corner and yellow," volunteers Syd.

"If you had a TV it could be black and white," says Peter.

"Yeah, you could talk about colors," adds Henry.

This is not quite where Mr. Greg wants the children to go, so he scaffolds with another question to set up for the key question he will later ask about their character's place.

"OK," says Mr. Greg, "if you walked into this portable, what would you say to describe it?"

Here Mr. Greg is using questions to guide the children in thinking clearly and describing closely. Learning to pay attention to details, to make what you are thinking more social so others can share it is such a critical part of learning how to live with others, as well as exercising skills like use of vocabulary and descriptors.

"It's the BEST in the universe!!" says Wes.

"Cool and with a piano," adds Nino.

"Big Time, our bunny," points Bart.

"Small and stuffy," sniffs Clara.

"Oh, paper people and astronauts on each end of the room," smiles Juanita.

"Shelves we built," adds Rita.

"Good," encourages Mr. Greg. "This is helping narrow down which portable."

Syd says, "Wetland school with a really old stove in it."

"Details may or may not help us to know which portable," says Mr. Greg.

Clara adds, "It has a 'hot seat.'"

Peter offers, "It has an ugly teacher!"

Peter sees an opportunity to throw down the glove, but Mr. Greg knows he is testing him. The other children watch this play out.

Mr. Greg looks at him and asks, "Do you want to base your description on something that can move? And on a value some people may or may not agree about what you call ugly?"

"OK," concedes Peter, "then it has a messy front desk because the teacher makes it messy." *Peter still pushes towards insult.*

Mr. Greg looks over at the desk, "Yes, there is a messy desk." *Well, some might describe Mr. Greg's desk as messy. As a teacher, though, I see order amidst the piles of paper and clutter.*

And Peter continues, "You *could* say about where it is on the outside: Wetland school in a portable closest to Sunny Street." *Now Peter begins to participate more openly.*

"Yes," responds Mr. Greg, "different pieces are details." *Mr. Greg responds to Peter and affirms his thinking.*

Mary grins, "Cool teacher and cool kids!"

Wes who has been sitting trying to figure out what detail is vivid enough lights up with a thought, "I bet *I* could find our portable! It is the one with worms under it!!"

Yes, this portable does have a worm farm the children planted under the porch. When it rains, long, undulating pinkish worms crawl onto the sidewalk in front of the porch. You have to watch your step!

"Let's read some of our descriptions we wrote last week that describe our room. Remember we were to use five sentences that gave us a picture of what your room is like. As I read the description, be thinking about what we know about this room. What information helps you know about this place, OK? Let's try it out."

Mr. Greg takes out a piece of paper and folds it "the hamburger way." You'll draw a picture of this room just from what you hear. Draw it as I read it. I'll say it a couple of times so you can catch all the words."

Here is a teacher who wants to assure all his students that they will not be left behind if he goes too fast, or in the case of folding the paper, he demonstrates as well as gives clues to the children so they can do it, too. I remember being in class where my teacher gave instructions once about how I was supposed to fold my paper or write my name. This became an ordeal, since I had a small (but not insignificant) learning disorder that makes translation of directions into an act of torture for me. I noted how I followed right along with Mr. Greg, and also noticed how not one of the children seemed to be impatient with either his paper demonstration or his reassurance that he would repeat the descriptions of the rooms. When Wes and Le did fall behind because making each letter took so long for them, all they had to do was look up and Mr. Greg repeated for them what they still had to write. This was done while the other children were writing. The dictation was done without much discomfort for any child, though this classroom has children who work at many different levels.

For the next half hour, Mr. Greg reads descriptions the children wrote about their rooms. The children are drawing what they envision from the words, and they are absolutely still, fully listening. Mr. Greg is reading *their* descriptions of *their* rooms.

After Mr. Greg reads three descriptions he tells the children, "Now on the fourth panel of your paper draw your room with an arrow at the bottom of whichever way LEFT is for you."

Again, everyone gets drawing. Soon they turn to their partners and begin explaining their rooms, using directionals and other particular descriptive clues. To an outside observer, this might look like a math lesson or a social studies project or a science mini-lab rather than a methodical storymaking by the class. *Storyline provides a contextualized setting and organization within which both teacher and students can operate with consistency and predictability, setting the foundation for new learning, making it safe to think about something (or someone) differently.*

Mr. Greg has invited to the classroom a guest speaker, a 16-year-old young woman who had been homeless and on the streets of Seattle for about two years before she found her way to the Halfway House where she now lives. Beth agreed to come talk to the children about how she felt to be homeless. Since I had to teach a class when she would visit, I asked the children to please pay attention so they could describe her visit to me and share what she said.

Frequently it is the habit of teachers to bring in "experts" as a way of introducing a topic to students. One of Storyline's principles is to build on the students' prior knowledge and experiences for all of the Storyline, so that concepts are both made explicit as well as changed during the episodes and dialogue. Only at the end of a Storyline does a teacher bring someone (or take his students to someone) who has both knowledge and experience to speak with the class. This presents a genuine opportunity for the students to engage the speaker in a discussion that is more reciprocal than one sided, for now the children are knowledgeable, too, and highly interested in hearing someone who has more to tell them about the topic, and who will respond to their questions with the seriousness they deserve. Beth will offer the class her own firsthand experience of being homeless for two years. Now that she is in a group home and has gone back to school, she feels it important to talk to children about what she has gone through as a way of encouraging them to work through their problems, not run away from them.

So I return the next day eager to hear about Beth and her talk. Since there was a change in the school schedule and the children were just going out on the playground for recess, I tagged along with about six children who gave me information all at once. Here is what I pieced together from the anecdotes they shared.

Beth came to visit them and she said it had been a long time since she was in a school like this. She told how she was living in a Halfway House for homeless teenagers. Ron, Bart and Sal, whose characters were the ones who had weapons, raised their hands to ask if she had ever robbed anyone. Beth told them that she was not proud of what she had to do on the street and that she wanted to put all that behind her. Raymond persisted and asked her if she had ever stolen a car and how had she done that. Beth said she had never stolen a car, and she wanted to talk about what she wants to do with her life now. "That's when it got really interesting," said Clara. "Beth told about how she wants to finish high school so she can go into music. She wants to sing. So we all got real excited and kept saying, 'sing for us, sing for us.' And she got real embarrassed but she went over to the piano and played and sang and she was sooo good. We all clapped and clapped and said thank you again and again and, you know what, she got tears in her eyes." We reached the stairs to the playground and my companions took off to claim the jungle gym bars and the swings, leaving me alone, wishing I could have met Beth and been there with the class.

Back in the classroom after recess, Mr. Greg and I spend some time on encouraging the children toward rich, thick descriptions of place. We will be asking them to draw where their homeless person spent last night in Seattle. We do not know how well the children know the city, but suspect that collectively they may have a good idea of it.

"What is our city like?" I ask aloud. "Imagine a place in the city. What is it like? Can you tell me about where you imagined?"

"Bars"
"Lake Forest Park with McDonald's and car lots"
"Suburbs"
"Fast Food Restaurants—Burger King, Burger Queen, Wendy's, Mc. . . ."

I never knew there were so many fast food restaurants in this city, but the list kept growing.

"Underpass"
"Tall and short buildings"
"Alleys"
"Stores, offices, places"
"Schools"
"Fields and parks and lakes"
"Camps, like Camp Long in West Seattle"
"Space Needle"
"Monuments and cemeteries"

The children's concept of our fair city is one of fast food, inhospitable buildings, and landmarks. Few reveal any personal sense of the city, such as parks or neighborhood. This is the city the children know: full of fast food, tall buildings, and the Space Needle. Later in the spring, Mr. Greg will have the children learn about their city through a series of day trips: urban excursions.

Mr. Greg hands out large butcher paper and drawing pens. "Can you sketch a map of where your homeless person spent a night in the city? You know, where he or she sleeps. Put in details so you can help us imagine what it was like."

Twenty-five minutes later even after the lunch bell rings, the children are still with their partners, drawing the place in the city where their homeless character spent the night. In a day or two, these drawings will be added to the growing artifacts of the homeless Storyline that were now hanging all over the room. Along with the displays, the children's homeless journal now has about thirty-five or forty pages of their writing, alongside their classmates, all typed by Mr. Greg. This is the reader they use during reading time in the day. They read from their own words, typed without misspellings, so they can see how words are spelled and sentences punctuated. At the end of the school year, children take this home with them. Do they reread it, I wonder? Mr. Greg tells me that their Storyline characters and these Storyline readers are always taken home by the children at the end of a Storyline, rarely do they leave them. Hence, I count on not having original artifacts to include in my field notes, only descriptions and copies, if the children will allow me to xerox their work.

The characters themselves have their place on the north blackboard, under the shelf which I was informed the children and a couple of parents had built early in the fall. Each character has a fully articulated face, filled in with all sorts of details. Some have colored chalk rubbed over their faces lightly to simulate dirt. Another has yarn combed into hair. Dorothy has two beautiful cats next to her. And everyone calls the characters by their correct names, conversing throughout the day about certain relationships or events that involve them.

As the Storyline has now gone on for a couple of months, I know that it is soon to draw to a close. The Food and Clothing Drive for earthquake victims in Kobe has been a schoolwide success. Even though it is over, children at Wetland school are still bringing in blankets and cans to the main office. There might be another delivery to the Japanese Consulate if this keeps up. Plans for tomorrow include a case worker from the district who is to tell us about how our school district serves its population of homeless children. I work with a school that has a designated code[3] that until recently assigned a number next to a child's name which indicated he or she was homeless. This is no longer district procedure.

Early morning rain again. It's no wonder Seattle is known for its Rain Festival—January 1st to December 31st. Bumbershoot weather reflects what I feel. Today is my last day with the children and I will miss them very much. Just as I am a participant observer in their Storyline, so the children have become participant observers in my study of their story. The easy smiles, the calls for help with spelling or word choice, the friendly sharing of what went on when I was away from them, all this and more I have come to value about being with them.

I walk up the six stairs to the portable doors and am surprised to hear not a peep from within. Had they gone to the library? Were they outside? I open the door to a darkened classroom, with a video showing on the TV monitor, and the entire class riveted to the screen. The video is a documentary of homeless children and their families in our school district. Children as well as their teachers, their case workers, and parents talk about their perspective of being homeless and trying to go to school. Peter is quietly doodling on some paper, but each time someone on screen talks about "feeling sad" he looks up to see who is speaking. This happens frequently over the rest of the twenty minutes of the video. When a child speaks of crying, Peter cannot take his eyes off the screen. It is the same for many of the children. Even though Kim cannot see the screen, she is inclining her head to hear each and every word. She sometimes whispers to her neighbor to describe who is talking. Total attention from all.

Ashley Conder from HouseShare is the guest speaker today. *Mr. Greg has invited Ms. Conder to offer another perspective of homelessness to the class. She works as a counselor and liaison between the school district and homeless families and has responsibility for matching a school with the circumstances of a homeless child. She spends large amounts of time tracking where the children are living. Since they have no address or phone, if she must contact a family, she has to go to them. Mr. Greg has judged the time is right to have Ms. Conder hold a discussion with the children about this other angle. He has told Ms Conder only that the children have been studying about homelessness.* As the videotape draws to a close, she gives a nod for the lights to be turned on. Looking at the children, she waits a moment before asking,

"Tell me something in the video you never heard before."

Juanita says softly, "Homeless kids are teased."

Peter adds, "Well, some start out not homeless, then when they are homeless they understand."

"What do you mean?" Ms. Conder wants to know of Peter.

"There was the lady who had had a home, and then she got homeless with her kids. And she said on the TV that she can't 'push homeless people out of the way' anymore. She understands what it is like now."

Dana agrees, "Yes, she understands."

"Well," probes Ms. Conder, "what would we do if one of those homeless kids went to Wetland school?"

Tanya responds, "I'd invite them to my house and share our food."

Sally adds, "We could make room in our school for them."

Dana says "We could give stuff to them."

"Oh," replies Ms. Conder, "you might mean donation drives. Do you know what those are?"

A sea of hands wave to be called on to tell of the donation drive for the people of Kobe. Then some children recall how there was a canned food drive when the principal had challenged the school to fill up a big bin in his office and they did. And then he had to go around in a silly T-shirt all day long. *Ms. Conder is taken aback by the large response of the children to her question, but continues to probe.*

"Well, what kinds of things do you think these children might need?"

"Money" "Food" "Paper" come the responses.

Mr. Greg chimes in, "Yes, think about if you don't have any pencil or paper how you would get along in school." *Ms. Conder is nodding in agreement. She is surprised by how much the children are thinking about problems she has to deal with each day in her work with homeless children.*

"Homeless people lose things a lot," continues Ms. Conder, "because they don't have any place to store their belongings. They don't have one place."

Children are nodding and remembering how they kept misplacing their possessions because there was not one place to always keep them.

Mr. Greg looks at Tanya, "A number of our homeless characters were burnt out so they don't have any possessions at all. Annie's been burnt out, right?" Tanya says "Yes."

Sally adds, "When we went to Mexico, we saw lots of homeless people."

Dana builds on this remark, "There's probably lots of homeless people in Japan right now."

"Yes, but Annie has collected new stuff. I wonder if homeless people have pets?" muses Tanya.

Ms. Conder smiles at her, warmed by her own recollections. "Yes, I know a couple of homeless people where I live in the University District.

Rupert has a dog. In fact, Rupert goes through dumpsters and gets out all recyclable things and puts them on our step. He tells us, 'You need to recycle.' Donations are a kind of recycle. You give people what you don't use, but they can. Rupert has two dogs. His other homeless buddy has one."

Mr. Greg comments, "What if the homeless only have one set of clothes, so you can never get them washed and cleaned. . . ."

Tanya is still thinking about this new information and her character, Annie, who lives in a dump. She asks, "Do any homeless people you've met live in a dump?"

"Not any I have personally met," acknowledges Ms. Conder.

Juanita is scowling. "I heard about a person who was run over—they didn't see him."[4]

"Yes, lots of homeless people die because of accidents or poor health or lack of food," answers Ms. Conder.

Tanya volunteers, "My homeless character is Annie who lives in a doghouse in the dump."

Ms. Conder has been hearing about these people and finally asks, "Who *are* these homeless characters?"

The hands are raised so quickly (and so high) Ms. Conder seems to take a step back.

"Ting Tong is an inventor who messes around with electricity. That's why his hair stands straight up," says Clara.

Sally adds, "She just got home after she ran away because she had been abused. It was a scary experience. She had to go beg for money."

Chase says, "Brian is my character and he found an abandoned house."

"Boy, that is lucky," comments Ms. Conder, "It doesn't happen very often. Why do you suppose it is important to talk about the homeless?"

For many of the children the compassionate imagination they have developed by and through their characters is in full swing. Their comments are serious and there is a sober tone to what they are saying. The notion of homelessness—of being homeless—is no longer something that happens to somebody else. The children have had to struggle to figure out what to do about getting food, finding a place to sleep, feeling vulnerable. They answer her question with due seriousness. Their prior notions about homeless people have been articulated within the framework of Storyline; their experiences have now taken on new meanings as they have come to learn about what it means to be homeless.

Kim speaks first, "Because they are important."

Tanya adds, "They can get sick and die without food and water."

Sally says, "We want to help."

"To give back to people," Ms. Conder says, "feels good."

A chorus of voices say "Yes."

"Well," Ms. Conder continues, "part of what you can do to help the homeless is to talk about what is true. Do you know what a stereotype is? It is a false generalization. So don't let people say 'All homeless are dirty,' or 'All homeless want to be dirty.' "

"Wait," says Wes, "you want us to tell people homeless people aren't dirty?"

"Yes," answers Ms. Conder, "I want you to tell people that homeless people are individuals and unique. They are people just like us."

Mr. Greg reads aloud from a *New York Times* article a few weeks old about a homeless woman who lives in New York's Kennedy Airport. "For four years," Mr. Greg reads, "this woman has lived at Kennedy with her cart, luggage, make-up, two shirts, and two sweaters. She gets her mail delivered to the chapel where the chaplain holds it for her. She says here in this interview, 'I feel safe here. This is my home.' There are about a dozen homeless at Kennedy. It's different than living on the streets or in parks. They blend in here at the airport; they blend in with travelers. No aggressive panhandling." Mr. Greg looks up, asks if they know what that means, and then finishes, "Airports are safer than other places for homeless. And some people don't have a choice."

The class has been giving intense attention for over fifty-five minutes now, and recess is almost here. As Mr. Greg and some children say goodby to Ms. Conder, I go over to the back table and take a seat. Le and Wes come bouncing over to me. Wes looks at me and says, "I useta think I knew all about homeless people. . . ."

The bell rings and we all begin to walk out into the sunshine of a winter's day.

Notes

1 The names of teacher, students, and the school have been changed to conceal identity. See appendix A for a brief history of Storyline's development.

2 Katherine Paterson. *A Sense of Wonder: On Reading and Writing Books for Children*, New York: Plume Books, 1995, 207.

3 This code has been eliminated from district reporting, so there is now no discriminating identifying number next to the homeless child's name. No one at the building or administrative level knows who or who is not homeless by looking at the printouts for schools. However, schools are trying to be responsive to the special needs of the homeless, and case workers, counselors, and other support staff all work together at the building level once a child is found to be from a homeless family. The approach of schools, such as B.F. Day, in Seattle, is to work with the entire family to help the child remain in one place long enough to continue going to the same school. Within the last few years, children who are homeless can attend any school, regardless of their address, thus allowing potential for continuity. See Sharon Quint's *Schooling Homeless Children.*

4 A few months ago the media reported that a homeless man was run over as he slept in an alley. The driver did not see him.

Chapter 2

Trust and Education: Trust as an Aim and Means of an Educative Community

Mr. Greg and his class of third graders are continually learning many ways of relating to one another and to the world they live in. Even the children's homeless characters are included, treated with the same seriousness of respect and recognition offered all participants in this classroom. Mr. Greg demonstrates two basic tenets of fostering trust in our classrooms: through listening and through dialogue. Later in this chapter, we will examine a classroom incident where the participants' relationships knowledge this respect and recognition both in words and in actions.

In this chapter, I conceptualize trust as an outgrowth of dialogic relationships, where the teacher is wholly present[1] in listening to students, recognizing and respecting their agency. Through listening and engaging in participatory relations, the teacher locates the starting place through those themes and topics that students discuss. In gaining their interest and attention, the teacher guides students into habits of inquiry, dialogue, and into a companionship of learning together. It is through those themes and topics students can become engaged with that provide the aims and means of an educative community, where teaching the curriculum is part and parcel of paying attention to students as complex, capable, growing human beings.

The notion of trust among and between the participants is foundational to an educative community. How trust is fostered is not something we as teachers can do by direct instruction, just by telling our students. Rather, trust must be developed through our actions, behaviors, and attitudes expressed in the day to day living together of teacher and students.

Most important here is that this particular type of trust encourages participants to see one another as individual persons, complete with thoughts, experiences, desires, and their own unique ways of looking at the world. Further, students develop trust when they are treated as subjects worthy of respect and recognition of others, not as objects or empty vessels.

To understand the role of trust, I draw from Martin Buber and John Dewey and argue that trust engendered in the interpersonal relationships between teacher and student, student and student, promotes an educative experience, and as such is the aim and means of an educative community. Dewey helps us distinguish between what is educative and miseducative within the culture of the classroom. Buber helps us understand our notion of trust by discussing three types of dialogic relationships, two of which help to illuminate our notion of trust. Through understanding these types of dialogue we can conceptualize a notion of trust that is developed over time. Further, I will develop a sense of what classroom culture might be when trust is present.

To determine just what allows trust to flourish in a classroom, we must look to its underlying foundations. Trust must be developed and cultivated on a continuous basis among all participants in the classroom; it cannot be dictated. Otherwise, it becomes superficial, much like the polite behavior that students are daily reminded about, but so frequently ignore in school. Multidimensional, trust is developed and cultivated through the spirit and complexion of the relationships within the classroom. In what ways can dialogue foster trust in our classrooms?

Shared understandings and meanings within an educative community are made possible through dialogue. As Dewey argued, "Communication is a process of sharing experience till it becomes a common possession."[2] In the course of communicating shared experience, relationships are interactive, based upon dialogue and, in an educative community, marked by mutuality and inclusion, that is, a reciprocal exchange of understandings and coming to make sense of the world together.

For trust to flourish in a classroom, the quality of the relationships between teacher and students and among students must be open and respectful, especially of difference, which must be nurtured, not flattened. To cultivate a climate of respect, recognition, and openness, a particular kind of dialogue needs to be fostered—one where the student knows he or she is listened to, and where the teacher continually tries to understand what the student means. Buber describes this particular dialogue where persons strive to hear others in order to understand them and to find connections that link them in relation to one another.[3] What I think he means is that we cannot shut out our students or shut off ourselves when students speak with us, even when what they may say to us is uncomfortable or grates against our value system. We have experienced the discomfort of hearing students confront our beliefs, and therefore our images of ourselves as "teacher." Yet, we need to engage with our students for it is through this dialogue that students and teacher come to know and understand one another. Yes, this is problematic when our students come to us with little or no experience in being listened to, much less engaged in the kind of dialogue that fosters respect and recognition. These situations, where students display a lack of respect and unwillingness to listen to one another, are too common in our schools. And that is even more reason why the teacher should welcome and listen to students' ideas and experiences, use these as the foundation for posing problems, demonstrating other ways of relating, and selecting topics that engage and interest students. Trust's underpinnings, then, have a source in deep beliefs about teaching and learning of the teacher, who in an educative community, is as much a participant as a person who leads the students, yet retains the responsibility for the learning, the teaching, and the environment in the classroom. Let us turn to the first example Buber has of dialogue: monologue disguised as dialogue.

When the teacher is viewed as the sole source of knowledge for his or her students, a one-sided dialogue takes place: the teacher talks and the students listen or answer the teacher's questions. This monologic dialogue can lead to miseducative experiences for students. Charles Dickens's satire *Hard Times* describes a teacher and his class in industrial London mid-1800s. Mr. Gradgrind, the headmaster, gives instructions to the new teacher, a one Mr. Choakumchild, to fill his charges with "Facts, sir. In this life, we want nothing but Facts." Looking at the rows of children seated with hands folded, Gradgrind and Choakumchild "swept their eyes [on] the inclined plane of little vessels then and there arranged in order, ready to have imperial gallons of facts poured into them until they were filled to the brim."[4]

One of Mr. Gradgrind's first demonstration lessons was to ask a girl student, number twenty, to describe a horse, since her father worked with horses (an unseemly job). The girl, Sissy, who knows a world about horses, upon being grilled by the stern Gradgrind, could only stammer and shuffle, not knowing how to reduce such a creature to bits and parts. Losing patience immediately, Gradgrind calls on the boy Bitzer to describe a horse, leaving Sissy to her humiliation. The description Bitzer gives is exactly what is wanted: a series of facts, critical attributes of the creature, horse. "Quadruped. Graminivorous. Forty teeth, namely, twenty-four grinders, four eye-teeth, and twelve incisors." The list went on from head to tail. All correct as a collection of "facts."

This script leaves no room for dialogue because only the teacher is knowledgeable. Children are not seen as substantial human beings with ideas and capabilities; rather, they are models of deficits needing to be filled with "imperial gallons of facts," meant to fix their state of deficiency. No where in this scene is there room for these persons who come to us as our students with diverse cultures, languages, feelings, interests, experiences, and perceptions: wholly complex human beings. Indeed, names give way to numbers, depending on the row and seat where the student sits (not unlike test scores used to place children in differentiated classes). Pouring information into the heads of students leaves little room for developing the kind of inquiring mind and critical thinking we need in our democracy. Instead only students' memorial ability is invited into the learning process. No room here for anything but the facts; the course is already fully decided on in the teacher's mind.

While this scene was meant to satirize the education delivered in Dickens's time, it is all too familiar to many of us in the classroom. The emphasis on facts is still with us. And to measure our storehouse of facts, schools rely on the achievement or proficiency tests administered at regular yearly intervals. Students' knowledge of facts is not the only thing these tests measure; they are also used to evaluate how "good a job" a school or a particular teacher might be doing with pupils. Do they know their facts? Walk into any bookstore and in the children's section can be found books for parents, telling how to build a child's IQ, what every first grader should know, how to get a preschooler to read. The quest for facts for their own sake is with us today. Sissy's storehouse of knowledge from her personal experiences with horses is discounted and ignored in favor of facts and objective descriptors of the quadruped.

I am not here to argue that facts in and of themselves are unnecessary to school and to learning. But the quest for facts as a substitution for understanding and knowing cripples this particular lesson. In our Gradgrind example, facts are ends in themselves, giving students little or no opportunity to develop their thinking about horses. Sissy's (and how many others who sat quietly in rows) understanding of the concept horse was rich and broad. John Dewey claimed that the dualism of mind and body, this separation between what we know and how we know it, twists and separates our practical understandings of our dynamic experiences into discrete categories of lists and facts. He warns that when educators fail to use the concrete experiences of their students there is danger of creating miseducative experiences; that is, we make future experiences less accessible or meaningful, even inhibiting to students. Then experiences can depress students' motivation to learn and their power to understand or meet future experiences with open minds. Learning, if viewed as a collection of facts, is determined by the one in power, the teacher, as something in isolation, independent of student concepts, understanding, and experiences.

In *Democracy and Education,* John Dewey described how education must be based upon the needs and habits of those who were being educated. To touch the students' interests is to engage and influence, to stimulate students to learn and strive to make sense of what they are learning. This is a dynamic place both for students and for the teacher. Such a place would have a teacher fully aware of herself or himself and her or his students, attentive to the needs, desires, and capabilities both of individual children and her or his class as a whole. In this dynamic place, learning is connecting the students with what is to be understood, not independent of their interests and capabilities, but based upon them. The learning of facts or pieces of knowledge for its own sake is regarded by the teacher as a weakened sense of education. A more holistic approach is warranted whereby the teacher uses her students' experiences and interests to generate understanding about its connection with our lives. Dewey argues against giving subject matter to students for them to learn disconnected from their own experiences. Rather, just the other way around, education should build upon the students' experiences to foster connection with what is being taught.[5]

In such an environment as Dewey warns of and Dickens describes, knowledge is mistaken as that which is spoken by the teacher as authority, leaving little or no room for trust to develop between participants. Instead, students are constantly judged by the teacher who is the authority. Students, especially students like Sissy, are alienated and often humiliated by the extrinsic criticism of the teacher. What naturally occurs out of such a climate is the silent, resentful student. And it is this silence that Dewey would mark as an indication of miseducative experience.[6] The dialogue so necessary for an educative community is developed through respect for all members and is based upon the belief that coming to know something worthwhile cannot be done out of its social context, even with all its attendant individual aspects.

Buber argues for a dialogue based upon relationship, where one is always aware of the other, different from oneself, but with whom one reaches to communicate. This is the dialogue of reciprocity and connection.[7] Dialogic relations form the basis of an educative community. Mr. Greg's class will help illuminate what trust looks like in a classroom.

The first aspect of the genuine dialogue is one of the mutual experience of inclusion. In brief, this inclusion is between two people who see one another as a subject, as one worthy of attention. There is no reduction here of one person to some category or a dismissal because of difference in outlook or nature, but a recognition that our life is connected to the other, each of us reflects the other as a subject, not an object.[8] We can discover this in the exchange between Peter and Mr. Greg. Recall that Mr. Greg had asked the children how to describe the portable they were in. Peter offers, "It has an ugly teacher!" Mr. Greg did not respond in kind to Peter, though this might have happened with another teacher. But for Mr. Greg, Peter's rough edges are part of Peter at that moment. Telling Peter not to insult or make sarcastic remarks would maybe, just maybe, last for a short while until Peter is inspired to make a caustic comment again. This is not what Mr. Greg does. Mr. Greg has watched Peter since the first day, thinking about what he does and how he relates not just to him, but to the other children in class and on the playground. Mr. Greg does not retort in kind to Peter, regardless if they are on the playground or in class. He treats Peter the same wherever they happen to be, and that is with the open mind of respect. Recall in the exchange how Mr. Greg allows for Peter to come back to a place of respect for his teacher, when he could have so easily been trapped in a corner of his own making.

"It has an ugly teacher!"

Mr. Greg looks at him and asks, "Do you want to base your description on something that can move? And on a value some people may or may not agree about what you call ugly?" [Such responsive questions move Peter, and the others in class, to think about the description in a more critical way. He accepted Peter's answer, now he is offering some critical questions to clarify Peter's viewpoint. Being taken seriously, Peter amends his answer.]

"OK," concedes Peter, "then it has a messy front desk because the teacher makes it messy." [Peter won't quite give it up. He seems to be testing Mr. Greg, which he does often.]

Mr. Greg looks over at the desk in the back of the room, piled with children's papers and projects as well as other teacher paraphernalia. "Yes, there is a messy desk." [They can both agree on this point. Mr. Greg sees from Peter's point of view and acknowledges agreement not for the sake of appeasement or to subvert conflict, but to respond with honesty and accord to Peter's comment.]

And Peter continues, "You *could* say about where it is on the outside: Wetland school in a portable closest to Sunny Street." [Now Peter is coming back in as a participant of the group's construction of accurate descriptors of the classroom.]

"Yes," responds Mr. Greg, "different pieces are details." [Consistent in his voice and manner, Mr. Greg responds and affirms Peter's deeper description of the portable.]

This example with Peter also reveals the second aspect of Buber's dialogic relation. In this form, the teacher has awesome responsibility to maintain the paradox of being at once the teacher but with his idea of the pupil, from the student's perception. The teacher must be completely present for the student, yet at the same time with the student, what Buber describes as inclusion, attention given the student in such a way as to guide the student to reciprocate at some level that which the teacher gives.[9] For Buber, educating and being educated, the teacher and the student, is one situation on a continuum, the teacher at one end, the student at the other. The teacher must be entirely present—honest, authentic, seeking—and aware of the reality of the student, in this case, what Peter was doing by leading Mr. Greg into a place of disrespect and confrontation. Mr. Greg did not get pulled into a response that was on the same personal level that Peter cast at him. Mr. Greg is bound to his students, Peter included. Mr. Greg did not react to Peter, he responded to him, seeking to draw him out of his position of disconnection and disrespect.

In Mr. Greg's classroom, students are in the presence of a teacher who constantly works to understand them, comes to know them well, so that when they are themselves disrespectful or rude (as some might conclude Peter was in this instance) Mr. Greg continues to take them seriously, rejoining with a query about Peter's question. "Do you want to base your description on something that can move? And on a value some people may or may not agree about what you call ugly?" These queries leave plenty of room for Peter to think about what he is saying, perhaps even become aware of his motive for saying what he did.

In this instance, the dialogue between Peter and Mr. Greg also brought to light the limits Mr. Greg himself places on his authority. He did not use his power as a teacher to silence Peter. He did continue to call on Peter, and subsequently a number of other students, to construct a description together woven from the threads offered by Peter. With patience, Mr. Greg built on his student's personal experience and opinion to help lead him to develop some critical understanding of this description. Mr. Greg was not filling empty vessels with imperial gallons of facts, rather, he was using the students' thoughts and speech as a basis for developing critical thought and habits through the socially constructed description. Buber tells us that in relations where there is a power differential, such as between a teacher and a student, the teacher must keep to the student's reality, rather than responding arbitrarily.[10]

Additionally, we see here echoes of Deweyan notions of experience and knowing. Mr. Greg is making use of concrete experiences and understandings of his students, rather than isolating the way they learn from what they learn. The dialogic habits he practices reveal to his students his respect for them, their thoughts, and their feelings. By situating the theme of homelessness they brought into the classroom as the topic to study, Mr. Greg connected the students' personal experiences and beliefs with a larger social issue. Using this topic, Mr. Greg gave the children's experiences a depth, an articulation, and visibility within the classroom. He brings these out into the open where their beliefs and experiences could be discussed as they were revealed through their characters, their characters' biographies, and by their own writing in their journals. However, for a teacher to present such a topic, unorthodox in most schools, as well as many other generative themes raised by students, requires a particular kind of relation, one where there is the constancy of being wholly present, that is, where the teacher understands his students and engages in genuine dialogue with them. The teacher listens to his students and responds to them genuinely and honestly. In turn, they learn that communication is not one way, like Sissy giving back facts to Mr. Gradgrind.

In this participatory setting, the students learn that each of them comes with understandings and ideas that they can share in writing and in speech without fear of being judged in a capricious way by their teacher. They also learn that the teacher asks questions and listens carefully to how they respond. This is what Buber was describing when he wrote about dialogic relations. Through emerging trust, students and teacher can create understandings in a search for new ways of being and knowing. This topic of homelessness generated a wealth of dialogue in class and out of it about the homeless, as well as written expressions in stories and narratives about their homeless characters. Using the students' narratives as the basis for the reading lessons was an effective tool to develop habits of critical inquiry. It was a way of understanding as much about themselves and about their beliefs and fears as it was about coming to understand homelessness.

Buber delineates different types of dialogue, from the monologues of Mr. Gradgrind to the mutually respecting genuine dialogue of Mr. Greg. A monologic life is one where all our conversation is carried on within ourselves, not made public for discussion or revision. We talk at each other, but we actually are speaking only to ourselves. This is a distortion of the type of communication we need in our schools and for our democratic life together.[11]

Buber goes on to distinguish between this monologue and two other types of dialogue, a technical dialogue we use when we need to communicate some particular knowledge and "objective understanding," a dialogue that seems to belong to our modern society. But the dialogue that is the dialogue of life is found when one is present to another. A dialogic life is the reciprocal sharing of one's ideas and attention, dynamic because it's always moving back and forth between the discussants. It's this back and forth movement that contrasts with the rigid speech of Mr Gradgrind and his class. It is this being present and real with the other that is missing from our little scene of teachers and "vessels," waiting to be filled with facts. Gradgrind even calls on the children by their seating number, "Child number twenty." Absent is any relationship other than authority and imposition. It is a world fragmented into discrete bits of facts that stand for the object itself, "Quadruped. Graminivorous." The dialogue we are presented in this story is parallel with the monologue, the one-sided talking, of which Buber warns. The danger here is that we can think we know, say a horse, without knowing it at all, that is, without linking the creature that we call horse with any experience we may have had. Once Bitzer gives back the list of horse attributes to Mr. Gradgrind, that is it. The facts speak for themselves and the only thing left is to be sure the other students conform their facts on horse with the teacher's. The one child present who truly knows what magnificent, strong creatures horses are, is struck speechless and mute by the teacher's demand for a recitation on the facts of the horse. Her experiences are so broad and deep, she hardly knows where to start to describe a horse. What type of horse? For what use? How many hands high does it stand?

There is no dialogue allowed in Gradgrind's class. There is no inclusion or reciprocal relation between any of the participants. With the invalidation of Sissy's experiences and understanding of horses the relationship between teacher and student is made sharp and distant: he knows and she does not. The teacher is the ultimate authority. Insinuated into this way of relating between teacher and student is also another level, that of the relationship the student has with what she knows. But not all teachers are a Mr. Gradgrind. Many teachers want sincerely to share their love of learning with their students. Many teachers do not want their students to learn facts, but truly seek to help them understand the subject, yet are required to cover large amounts of material in the school year, forcing teachers to adopt a "let me tell you, and you listen" approach. Zero degrees of freedom to deviate and negotiate around the objectives or syllabus and lesson force out the space needed to foster teacher-student communication that is respectful and mutual in nature.

To teach through listening contradicts how many educators view the teaching act. We must resist the temptation to view our students as blank slates or as deficient, incomplete persons, quite apart from what knowledge they bring into the classroom that may not count as "school learning." Though our Mr. Gradgrind presents a harsh example, nevertheless, even likable and kind teachers can fall into believing that curriculum is static, what is worth knowing is what the teacher has been told to teach, waiting to be told or transmitted or presented to the waiting vessels we call our students. Even teachers who smile, clothed with good intentions, can hold monologues. To make the leap into dialogue demands an internal shift in a teacher's beliefs about teaching and learning. The teacher needs to be willing to step into the dialogic space required to hear his or her students. And this dialogic space may take forms we as teachers need to translate. Before dialogue can happen in the classroom, the teacher has to listen. Here is the story of how one teacher came to this insight.

This is a story about a warm and spirited woman in her retirement years. When asked if she would share with me a story that would offer me an idea of the kind of teacher she was, she smiled and gave herself over to the memory of a day that she described as nothing short of transformational. She had, she told me, graduated from a prestigious teachers' college in the east. The college "armed me with the latest pedagogy and I was eager to shed light into the minds of my charges." Upon graduation, she found a position in a large urban city in the east:

> I was given a third grade class, as anxious about me as I was about them. It took many weeks to train the children in my expectations of normal school behavior. I had so much to teach them, no time must be wasted in misbehavior. The days became routinized, and with relief I could count on their little faces looking intently at me as I would present lessons in history, mathematics, English, and, on this day, science.
>
> This lesson on the solar system was one I had spent an extra amount of time writing. Visual aids included a grapefruit; that put me over my grocery budget for that week. Also were paper planets I had spent all weekend cutting out for this demonstration of how planets orbited about the sun (grapefruit). My solar system lesson had been based on one I had written for my teacher education professor. He had liked it very much, giving high marks for clear objectives, interesting materials, probing questions, and challenging activities. I just knew the children were going to get really excited about this!

> Well, I began that lesson with such enthusiasm. The children were at their desks, hands folded, awaiting, it seemed to me, enlightenment. And I began to teach them about the solar system. I had the grapefruit poised in the air with one hand, while the other hand juggled the paper planets. Actually, it was really masterful. So absorbed was I in my erudition I did not notice anything until I looked up, expecting to see grateful faces smiling with understanding. Instead I saw my third graders in a circle, rear-ends up, heads down, orbiting about something on the floor. The children had quietly slipped from their seats to look at—what I wondered.
>
> Within the next minute or two, a rush of emotion went through me. I was indignant that such a fine lesson, with hours of preparation and cost in my money and my time, should be ignominiously received by my ungrateful students. Yes, I was angry. And I was frustrated. And I was summarily ignored! I took a deep breath and went over to the circle of children on the floor.
>
> There in the middle of the circle was the culprit: a cricket. The children were so rapt in attention they did not notice I had stopped my elegant lesson on the solar system. They did not know I was there looking on. The cricket, oblivious to the drama, seemed actually to be comforted by the warm breaths surrounding it. It would walk a few steps, then wiggle its antenna and stop.
>
> And it struck me that here in this little solar system, the cricket had become the center of the children's universe. It came to me that I could be part of it or remain standing on the side, excluded from the wonder of their discovery and interest. My decision changed my teaching from that day forward. Why not join the children? Why not take from their points of interest and make their journey mine, too? The lessons I learned from that cricket served me and my third graders well. We initially studied crickets, writing about them, building little cricket cages for them, reading how crickets were viewed (or eaten) in other cultures. Our room chirped throughout the day and all year from the growing cricket population and from the children, whose interest only grew as they learned more and more about these little creatures.

We may ask, What did this teacher hear when she stepped into the dialogic space of the children's interest in the cricket? Where is trust in this story and what does it have to do with this particular listening? As she listened to the body language of her students, this teacher came to understand she could trust her students to *want* to know and learn. What they wanted to know about, crickets, she used to cultivate their engagement with a common interest, the first stirrings of an educative community. Any teacher would be stopped in her tracks if she could see her students so intently occupied observing and inquiring about a subject. In fact, it is what most teachers strive to create in their classrooms, intense interest and habits of inquiry. Using the topic of crickets allowed this teacher to direct that interest of her pupils toward investigation, discussion, writing, and reading about this common interest. Habits of inquiry and dialogue emerged as attributes of her classroom. The lively dialogue between the students led to exchanges of ideas and perceptions and the formation of new understandings about crickets, and a shared understanding of a common experience. The teacher was no intruder, no "depositor of facts, nothing but facts," or even a transmitter of knowledge about crickets. The very way she related to her pupils was changed. She took the perspective of her students. By doing so, the teacher saw her students' learning not as an extension of what she was transmitting through subject matter, but as a dynamic place for both her and her students. She saw learning from the standpoint of the student, and actively chose to pursue that learning with her students through taking their perspective. One of the conditions for dialogue, then, is for the teacher to truly listen to her students because she trusts they have something to say to her. From this dialogic stance emerges the reciprocity of listening—the teacher begins with listening to her students and in listening achieves both the attention of her students and the path to organizing the curriculum to meet the students at their point of entry, their interests and experiences. How powerful this is in a classroom! For this to have any chance of occurring, the teacher must be wholly present to her students, giving them her full attention. Our cricket teacher had to let go of what she thought was her job as a teacher in order to hear what it was her students wanted to learn. Crickets was the current topic, but she came to understand how such intense listening to the sound of the chirps was the intensity of engagement and interest from the children's point of view, not hers.

Let us revisit the paradox we have been discussing. Trust is a process, dynamic and on-going, rather than a quality we can tell students to do. We cannot, as teachers, demand or just tell our students to trust. Instead, we must trust ourselves to hear our students and through hearing them, guide and facilitate their direction toward learning. This process of listening, responding, and questioning is the democratic process of our society that can be learned through the types of sociality as we find in a classroom, where knowledge and beliefs and feelings are part of what it means to live together, with the potential to understand one another. It is with conscious effort that a teacher fosters such a climate. Through an educative community, trust develops between the participants through dialogue and participatory relations in the climate of respect and recognition. Where trust is present among students and teacher, there is potential for sharing of concepts and ideas that more authentically reflect the perceptions of those participants. An avenue toward encouraging this sharing is story.

In the next chapter, we turn to the power of story, because story and narrative help us make sense of the world and sense-making is an integral part of what makes an educative community. We will continue to probe understanding and being understood as part of an educative community, where trust is present. Following the chapter on story and narrative will be one that argues for a particular type of civility. The feeling heart of civility is based upon compassionate imagination and is constitutive to an educative community.

Notes

1 Martin Buber stresses the importance of being fully present with one's self while attending to another in *Between Man and Man* (21, 98, 101, 114). If one is to reach out to another, a teacher toward a student, for the purpose of being in dialogue with that student, a teacher must know himself or herself, be with himself or herself. If we are to truly hear our students, we must first be able to hear ourselves, be honest with ourselves. Such honesty or presence allows for what Buber describes as turning toward another, that is, being able to see the wholeness of another person, respected and recognized as a person with life experiences, coming to us (as our student) with beliefs, ideas, and all the complexity of a human being. Being truly present with another fosters mutuality, a reality between them, where the teacher does not use or manipulate the student for any reason, including to motivate her to do her schoolwork or learn the lesson. Buber's notion of responsibility of a teacher is far beyond that of teaching subject matter; instead, Buber views education as learning to be human together by influencing the character of our students. Such a notion of education demands another way of viewing teachers and the teaching act because it is based upon dialogue, the dialogue of mutuality and respect. The teacher must know her students in order to gain the understanding of what is needed in order to help them grow. This requires what Buber describes as the responsibility of a teacher. New York: Collier Books, 1965.

2 John Dewey, *Democracy and Education,* Carbondale, Ill: Southern Illinois University Press, 1916/1985, 12.

3 Martin Buber, 19.

4 Charles Dickens, *Hard Times*, New York: Penguin Books, 1854/1980, 12.

5 John Dewey, *Democracy and Education*, 114, 133, 136.

6 Ibid. Dewey makes the point that all experiences are not truly or equally educative. In education, we must be concerned about those experiences that promote this sense of new growth from our experience. 25.

7 Martin Buber, 20.

8 Martin Buber, 99.

9 I interpret Buber's use of the term "inclusion" to mean a particular kind of compassion or sympathy, but richer and deeper, where a person extends his or her own reality to experience an event felt from another's point of view, living through our imagination from the view of the other. This is the basis of a dialogical relation, where two persons are able to be real, genuine to one another. Since Buber argues that pure dialogue is the relation in education, inclusion is a critical term if we are to understand how Mr. Greg responds to Peter, paradoxically understanding and accepting Peter, while at the same moment responding to Peter so that he can move from his place of disrespect for Mr. Greg. Martin Buber, 96–100.

10 Martin Buber, 99–100.

11 Martin Buber, 19–33.

Chapter 3

The Power of Understanding: Sense-Making as an Aim and Means of an Educative Community

Communication is the cornerstone of our social life and, by definition, education. Indeed, Dewey argues that communication enlarges our vision and capacity to understand as well as fosters growth. But as we discussed in the last chapter, we must pay attention to cultivating the type of communication that fosters educative experiences, to who speaks, what is said, and how we listen to one another. For an educative community, such communication is crucial to its very existence. Therefore, we turn to how we might encourage our students to communicate their thoughts and beliefs to one another, to speak with a public voice in the classroom, instead of silently retreating. A key way to help children share with one another is through story.

Mr. Greg supported his students to learn from one another and from their own experiences by eliciting stories, both their own and their characters. As stories were shared, students revealed how they were making sense of the world they knew. In sharing, they also gave advice and questioned each others' points of views, allowing Mr. Greg to ask critical questions for them to think about. As teachers, we are in significant positions to affect the lives of our students, to guide them to find their own individual centers of gravity, with the curriculum we choose, our interactions with one another, and through the stories we share together.

This chapter is about the role of story in an educative community. It is important to consider the role of story because that is a primary way that children make sense of the world.[1] However, to use narrative as a method for teaching requires a different role for us than one traditionally construed. (In this instance, narrative and story are meant to be synonymous, but whenever possible, I prefer to use story.) This chapter explores what happens when the role of the teacher shifts to invite story in the classroom to encourage students to make sense of their experiences and to share this sense-making with one another. The dimensions of coming to make sense of one's experience in a way that fosters personal, as well as social and intellectual growth for students, is a crucial measure of an educative community. To discuss this, we must examine the moral epistemological nature of narrative, communal ways of understanding through story, and the role of the teacher using this pedagogy. We begin with the role of the teacher.

In traditional education, the task of the teacher is to teach, students. This entails a teacher telling the students what they need to know to pass the class, to score high on achievement tests for the school or district, to measure up to the standards of the state learning goals. As a social studies teacher, I found out early in my career that in an academic year it was impossible to cover United States history from Columbus to the present day, even in rushed chronological order. Each year the textbooks I was required to use seemed to get thicker and the students more resistant to the "rush to cover" the curriculum approach my colleagues and I used. A democratic climate in our classrooms was not a topic of our faculty lounge discussions.

In such an environment, the scope of learning was contained in memorizing and mastering the subject; understanding and knowing were not made social, dialogue was absent as the main mode of communication between students and teacher. The directed demonstration and lecture allowed me opportunity to "teach" the subject as quickly and as efficiently as possible, leaving little or no room for student voice, except to ask a question or give a short answer to one. My job was to "teach" my students to learn and then describe United States history. Democracy was a word we learned to spell and defined for tests; it was a term found in our textbooks that was out there in the "real" world, but not something we experienced in school.

While both my students and I disliked what I had to do to them, except for a resistantly disruptive student or two, no one questioned this mode of teaching. I did not understand back then that their silence was a form of resistance, as well. Having been successfully socialized into education, my colleagues and I thought that this is what education was about. We did not question the assumption that the learning in our courses (and in our school) could be quantitatively measured in the tests we administered regularly, that learning was equated with an achievement test score. Discourse in the classroom was relegated to teacher talk. I was the one who had responsibility to know what I was to teach and to assess whether I had done so. "Remediate" was commonly used to describe failure: not the teacher's, but the student's.

Working with textbook language and themes wore me down very quickly, but I did not know where to begin to change either my teaching or how to adjust the subject matter so my students could relate to it. It was my students who intervened between me and this pedagogy. I began to listen to them before class and after, when we would rest from being teacher and students. In this more informal space between classes I started to understand that their way of learning did not jibe with the way I was teaching. Something was deeply amiss if what I worked so hard to do (and thought about all the rest of the hours I was not teaching) was not helping my students learn in ways that excited them or involved them beyond the routinized responses they were used to giving. It was I who was remediated as I began to listen and pay attention to my students, and as they helped me change my perspective on teaching, opening up the possibilities of coming to know something together in ways I had before neither experienced nor imagined. They illuminated for me what teaching might be by sharing their ideas and understandings about history and relating it to the reality of their lives, by telling stories, sharing stories, writing stories.

And one day I "got" it. We had spent an entire class period just talking together about one of the stories a student had shared of her experience as a stranger in a new land. During that dialogue between my students and myself, it dawned on me that we were delving into issues that made a great deal of sense to many of us, myself included, and that they were sharing that sense with their classmates in a way that was real to all of us in some way. My center of gravity shifted as I realized that I was coming at teaching from the wrong direction, in spite of all my good intentions. Instead of working so hard to help students fill up on "Facts, imperial gallons of Facts," I instead asked myself "How could I help my students learn in meaningful and memorable ways?" It seems fitting that my journey into what educative meant for both students and teacher began with a student's story.

Stories provide a common context by engaging students as part of a learning community which fosters discussion and dialogue. Thus, learning itself becomes communal, where different values and ways of being in the world are affirmed through stories. Through story we find our place in the world, have the potential to change our existing ways of seeing, and connect our lives with the reality of others. The writer Katherine Paterson claims that stories are windows into the human spirit.[2]

But this approach to teaching and learning is problematical for teachers because it contradicts the traditional teaching approach many of us were taught as well as the ideology, pedagogy, and epistemology that underlie those methods. One epistemological stance is the traditional: teaching subject matter to students with little or no regard for what they themselves might bring to the discipline. This is what I had begun thinking teaching was, early on in my career. This pedagogy was marked by the fragmented ways students came to "learn" with little or no involvement of self or connection to their lives. Such distance on the part of my students also kept us apart from one another. My role was defined; so was theirs. But when I began to listen to children, I realized there might be a different way of knowing, a way of understanding that is less distant and fragmented, and that encourages the making of connections between what is known and those who know it.

If we examine the way story fosters sense-making for students, then we are obliged to discuss what happens with the teacher, who traditionally is cast as the one held responsible for students "knowing." Our primary notion of education is based on making students the knowers of what is conceived about the world. Only secondarily is education viewed as a way to gain knowledge for self-understanding about one's place in the world. This distinction between what we know and its effect upon us as individuals is an important part of our discussion. For if story is a powerful way for children to make sense of the world and their place in it, then it is crucial that we encourage our students to articulate their story and listen to the stories of others to discover their differences as well as their connectedness. Stories have the power to ignite our interest, our imagination and our curiosity. Isn't this the energy we teachers seek to animate our students' need to know? Don't we want our students to learn in meaningful and memorable ways that lead to their growth and development as full participants in society?

To ignite a student's interest and pursuit of understanding, of wanting to know about something, there must be intrinsic, internal motivation. Someone, like me during my early teaching days, telling students how, even why, they must learn about a topic simply sidesteps the question of how to ignite a passionate involvement in learning that is waiting to happen within students. When teaching is done by a teacher, separated from the learning done by students, and a body of facts await (growing higher each year), there is no room for thinking about what all this has to do with another. We remain separate entities, each of us has our job. Such separation between subjects, students, and teacher leads us away from meaningful intersections that engender dialogue.

Dewey argues against this dualistic nature of people to think and act about life, and how that dualism reveals itself in how and what educators teach students.[3] Mind and body are seen as separate entities, with the mind recognized as the one organ that pertains to knowledge. Dewey argued that such dualism is fraught with danger for a democratic society. The self is divided from its physical and social world when attention is paid only to accruing knowledge. The emotions of human experience are not welcomed into this paradigm of learning. This has the unfortunate effect of separating what one learns from how we make sense of the world, as my students patiently taught me. Teachers fall back on fear and authoritarian methods to force some students to learn the subject, often through mind numbing drills and rote memorization.

In *Democracy and Education,* Dewey tells us human experience is strongly social and should not be separated from how we educate the young, particularly if what we are educating for is public life in a democratic society. Humans live in a community "in virtue of the things [we] have in common . . . beliefs, aims, aspirations and knowledge which afford us a common understanding." He goes on to argue that our "beliefs, aims, aspirations, and knowledge" cannot be physically handed over to the next generation nor told to them, but must be communicated over time through our society's institutions, one of which is school. Our entire social life is communication, Dewey says, and "[t]o be a recipient of a communication is to have an enlarged and changed experience."[4] Our social life demands teaching and learning for its own permanence. Living together educates because it enlarges and enlightens our experiences. Schooling, therefore, plays a significant role in the health and welfare of our society.

This enlargement is what we should be striving for in schools, that is, searching for occasions to reflect upon past experiences to make sense of meanings in our lives together. Dewey states, ". . . [I]n dealing with the young, the fact of association itself as an immediate human fact, gains in importance. . . . Since our chief business with them is to enable them to share in a common life we cannot help considering whether or not we are forming the powers which will secure this ability."[5] If the purpose of schools, its "chief business," is to enable our children to share in a common life now and in the future, then teaching and learning must be connected to their lives now, deliberate and situated in the themes and languages they bring to us as a way of illuminating their place in society. This is what I envision about how we might help our students relate personal growth to public life.

But in our complex society, direct telling and instruction about society becomes difficult, if not impossible. Not only is our population too large and pluralistic, but our knowledge base and technology are too great to transmit wholly intact to any one person. But, Dewey points out, "[f]ormal instruction (such as in schools) easily becomes remote and dead—abstract and bookish." He goes on to state that our society stores its culture in symbols. "There is the standing danger that the material of formal instruction will be merely the subject matter of the schools, isolated from the subject matter of life-experience."[6] Therefore, schools cannot ignore the "social necessity of education and its identity with all human association that affects conscious life, and which identifies it with imparting" these symbols "through the acquisition of literacy," in other words, communication both verbal and written. Further, "communication is a process of sharing experience till it becomes a common possession. It modifies the disposition of both the parties who partake in it." Written in 1916, Dewey's words ring with a present urgency when he writes,

> As societies become more complex in structure and resources, the need of formal or intentional teaching and learning increases. As formal teaching and training grow in extent, there is the danger of creating an undesirable split between the experience gained in more direct associations and what is acquired in school. This danger was never greater than at the present time, on account of the rapid growth in the last few centuries of knowledge and technical modes of skill.[7]

Education that leads children into public life requires a classroom where children's voices are encouraged and listened to. One way to encourage children's voice is through story. In a classroom where civility and trust invite students to share their experiences and beliefs with one another, story is one way of weaving in these experiences and beliefs together with strong skills, critical thinking and academic knowledge. In chapter 1 we noted how Mr. Greg drew stories from his students about their homeless characters' lives, and as they built their characters' biographies, so, too, did Mr. Greg formulate questions that encouraged them to clarify their own beliefs as well as the beliefs of others through a communal and participatory environment, marked by dialogue and respect.

Why should teachers create a space where children's stories are encouraged and heard? They should because in creating a place for children to speak through stories, educators might widen their students' perspective about their place in their school, their community, and in the world at large. Through the language of stories, children come to recognize their personal voice and, in that recognition, come to that still small voice within each of us that puts us in touch with who we are, with our center of gravity.

Creating an environment where voice is listened to intersects with the dialogic relations I discussed in the last chapter on trust. Dialogue and voice are intertwined. Before students can fully enter into a dialogue, there must be some validation for their own thoughts they share with us. Public discourse within the context of a classroom can prepare one for living in a multicultural world, where language use is varied and complex. And one place voice is located is in the variety and complexity of stories.

But for many of our nation's children and students, school serves to marginalize and silence their public voice, as it simultaneously invalidates their personal voice. Too often, particular lives are not cherished in schools, where efficiency for the many is given priority over recognition of the specific needs of teachers and students.[8] There is little or no room for exploration of those "aims, beliefs, aspirations and knowledge" that Dewey spoke of. In the next chapters, this experience of marginalization and membership that occurs in classrooms will be expanded as part of the discussion on fostering a sense of belonging, so vital to an educative community. But here we turn our attention to the epistemological nature of story.

Mr. Greg is a teacher who seeks ways to engage as many of his students as possible in observing, hypothesizing, discussing, sharing, and writing about what they know. Yet he also is aware that he must begin with deep ties between him and the students. He does not want to separate what they learn in school from their life outside of school, which we know often occurs. Rather, he wants to invite connections between their lives both in and out of school, and to expand, not limit, their communication with one another about themes that are important to them. To invite connections, Mr. Greg has to know his students. He can learn about who they are and what they think through their stories.

Teacher and author Karen Gallas wonders aloud for all teachers about the capacity our children have already to be creative learners and critical thinkers, but that their capacity is capped and redirected by us as we strive to teach for mastery, to teach about proficiency, and to "cover" all the stacks of curriculum we think we must teach each year.[9] She goes on to claim that stories that describe ways of living in the world make it larger than life and imbue our perception of what life can be for us that goes beyond the circumstances of the event itself. As Gallas points out, stories help children make sense of their experiences and the world. Stories help children see different models of living together from which they can better understand their own ways of being. The third graders give us vivid examples of this in their renderings of their homeless characters' lives. When the children began writing their characters' biographies, some incorporated the string of arson fires into their narratives as one explanation of how their characters became homeless. Some children used other situations, some based perhaps on imaginary fears or imagination or in their real life.

Recall that some homeless characters were "kicked out by their parents" or "their parents died because of cancer" or "their parents used drugs and got in jail." Mr. Greg accepted and took seriously each character's (and each student's) explanation, while at the same time encouraging the linkages in logic and fact that might have been skipped in the biography. In fact, it was the culture of this classroom to expect and rely on audience participation to build a character's story.

For example, when Jo introduced King Kong, who was "12 × 9 years old," and "older than the universe," many hands went up. This longevity of her character raised questions in the minds of her audience, and while Jo was unsure of herself at times, it was not out of discomfort with their questions and interruptions. She had, said Mr. Greg, been one of the more active questioners of her classmates during the astronaut Storyline, which she became quite interested in. Perhaps, I thought, she wanted to connect King Kong's character with her astronaut by making him "older than the universe" and "an alien." Many students were shaking their heads, though, trying to make sense out of Jo's description. A boy went over to the bookshelf to pull out a reference on the universe, just to make sure about what "older than the universe" might mean in terms of temporal measurement. As the audience we do not find it so easy to jump to conclusions about a character, not so easy as it is to jump to conclusions about someone who is sleeping in the park near our school. This distance, made possible by the character's story, allows us to think in more critical ways about someone. The teller, in this case, Jo, has a certain added power and importance when she recounts her narrative of King Kong. It is, after all, her vision of the world through King Kong, and it puts forth her point of view for the audience. The clarifying questions from the class added new levels of understanding to the narratives of all the characters. Some children changed their character's narratives to adjust to this exigency of the audience to make sense of the story. Just as the children were listening to Jo, so Jo was listening to what they were asking her without defensiveness or becoming silent. There is profound need in our society to listen to a variety of voices from the diverse communities in our country, each with a perspective to share.

In many schools, personal stories and particular lives do not have the value and weight in the prescribed curriculum. Imagine if you will a social studies textbook. One has only to read samples of pages and photos to get a sense of how hidden and reduced are the human particulars of any topic. How can students come to respect and value a particular life of a person if the images which are given them are of Everyman, yet of no one? Even if a child were to glimpse himself or herself in a text, such as a social studies book about cultures, that glimpse is often a composite or generalized representative that would be offered as a standard to compare with our own tradition. The photos that accompany such a textbook are deliberately chosen not to portray individuals, but portray prototypes of a group. Children learn little about a person's concrete existence through abstract texts, which tend to "flatten and reduce" the human story. The irony, then, is that such painful and expensive effort is given over to stripping away the very stuff of life, the particular human engagement of living and its connection with the topic in study.

In *The Boy Who Would Be a Helicopter*, Vivian Paley focuses on the place of storytelling in influencing the way preschool children come to know and understand themselves, each other, and the world they inhabit together. She reveals another way of banking knowledge that contrasts vividly with traditional pedagogy. Through the use of story she shows us ways of engendering wisdom as a source of power for self-understanding within a community. She uses story because stories provide opportunities for children to make meaningful connections between what they themselves know and what they are working on in school. In Paley's classroom, stories provide the connective glue of the classroom community, linking children to one another through the sharing of images and endings and allusions and ideas. The children create their joint story by sharing their own with one another. We saw much the same phenomenon in Mr. Greg's class, too, as the third graders shared their characters' biographies and experiences with each other.[10] Stories provide the space to build this literature together. Through story Jason (and his classmates, too) became open and receptive to new ways of seeing themselves and others. By cultivating respect for the stories they told, Paley showed that she heard each one's own frames of thought.[11] Paley, like Mr. Greg, listened to the way the children made sense of their lives. The primary, crucial task for the children, and I would say for all our students and their teachers, is making meaning, which Paley describes as the essential of teaching and learning. Her vision of the storyteller as one who builds culture within the classroom community allows us to see how every story the children tell connects with others and becomes a part of the community.[12] Through one story, many emerge and intertwine as a community of storytellers is formed. As we saw in Mr. Greg's class, as well, children's imagination is portrayed by their stories and characters, each sharing his or her authority by reciprocal listening, solidifying a feeling of trust and communal sense-making.

Jason, a loner and outsider in Paley's classroom, is a boy who, through stories—his own and his classmates—slowly becomes part of the community. His story is heard by his classmates, and he is included in their stories. Eventually Jason finds his place among the rest of the children, remaining Jason in all his quirkiness. Through the year, the children around Jason sought to involve him in their storymaking, and for a long period of time, his participation was through his imaginary helicopter persona. Through shared narratives that grew more expansive to include even helicopters, the community of children developed a common definition of who they were through collective narratives that they made themselves. Paley and Mr. Greg showed us how stories were like stones in the pond, rippling outward to reach all of the group as they build their story together—each a listener, each an author—all belonging, even those who are on the margins.

The power of story, then, provides an important dimension to our educative community: that of coming to understand another who is different from us. So far we have focused on the stories from the students themselves; however, literature can also illuminate our understandings of ourselves and others. Story forms a basis for deep understanding and provides a platform for discussion with those who differ from us. Stories have the power to move us to the heart, beyond our own story, and to connect with another through our imagination. In our society, we have wrought an educational system that is separate from emotion, exactly what Dewey warned against. If stories are used in classrooms then it follows that there is a place in actual learning, in engagement with knowledge and sense-making, where passion and emotion can potentially be a legitimate and powerful part of the curriculum. Stories acknowledge and legitimate feeling.

In stories, there is a place for feelings. Why is emotion important in education? Because this is where understanding about the world and life is fostered. Stories can help us hear the silence of another and respond. This is a lovely image and echoes the need for a feeling heart of civility I write about, the compassionate imagination that I think is vital to an educative community where the learner comes to know that through the knowing of another: internal insight which leads to understanding of the external. Children need to be conscious of their individual stories so they can engage in dialogue with those different from themselves. We learn that others are not extensions of ourselves, yet are deserving of sympathy.

We locate ourselves in the stories of others, finding the link between us. We can be moved by the story of another at the same time we are not persuaded or threatened by it. We learn that there is room in the world for difference. Unlike textbooks, which promote a unilateral view of the world, stories reveal the characters' conflicts, dilemmas, and struggles within a contextual framework. As in life, stories are often boldly biased, not hidden. Readers can feel sympathy without agreeing with a character's course of action, yet still feel the conflict and confusion. This stands in sharp contrast to the offerings in a textbook.

Amidst the differences that abound and surround us in our society, through story we can still hear the feelings and experiences of others and compare them to our own. Stories found in literature then help prepare children for new and unfamiliar ideas by linking their experiences and ideas with another's, albeit a character in a novel, but one built on understanding, familiarity, or respect.

Learning to recognize linkages is important to one's growth and development as a person. Though humans do share common experiences, we often fail to recognize them as such. While schools might emphasize social commonalties in before or after school activities, in classrooms we often revert back to the traditional stance of putting out facts to be learned and mastered. Strong skills and habits of inquiry are usually acquired alone; too much cooperation, in fact, might be construed as cheating. But without communal ways of understanding, we become like islands with no connection to that which we perceive as unknown or different. The use of stories in a classroom helps us perceive how our students conceptualize the world. This is a powerful force in learning and thinking that is often untapped and silenced in our classrooms when it could instead be encouraged and fostered.

Learning might then become a dynamic experience, at the same time both individual and communal. Such a different experience of learning would indeed lead to other ways of knowing and understanding, ones that would include others in what would otherwise have been an independent, isolating task.

Stories help place us, the reader, as part of the larger connected human experience. We find we want to talk with others. We want to know what others feel and think and experience. Stories invite us, even for a brief instant, into the heart or mind of another. The reader, adult or child, interacts and subsequently influences the story as it is read and internalized. When we can understand what others feel, a bridge is forged allowing us to cross over and meet another or for another to cross and meet us.

Jason's experience in Paley's classroom and the children and Storyline characters in Mr. Greg's classroom reveal the power of story to bring us together. In our collective experience of the text, the meaning of the text widens. It expands our collective consciousness about the issues within the text. In so doing, the reader finds that the "I" does not stand alone. The "I" becomes "We." There is a residue of the collective consciousness left within us as individuals that further connects us to our sympathy and to our community. This sense of the "we" is necessary preparation for our participation and engagement in public life.

Through stories, the center of gravity is shifted from teacher as sole authority and joins the child as inquirer. This shift in the center of gravity in a classroom is a profound one, for it shifts away from teacher as messenger of knowledge and the textbook as authority for wisdom. The shift is founded upon the assumption that children are capable of engaging in the internal literary conversation between themselves as reader, the author, and the characters. It assumes children have voices of their own. The underlying question of this shift is who or what is the source of validation in the classroom? Does it rest only with the teacher? Is it with only the students? Or does it mean we must rethink what we as educators are doing in schools? For me, these questions reveal a deeper obligation for teachers because when children's voices are heard, we must *act*. What will we do with what we hear our students say? How will we respond to them as persons, and to their ideas, however divergent from what we are used to?

For some, it may seem as if I am abandoning any authoritative role for the teacher, and instead, advocating the very excesses of education that Dewey argued against in *Experience and Education* and that occurred during the late 60s and 70s in the United States. But I am not. A freewheeling, do what you feel like classroom is not at all what I am inviting you to envision. Instead I am imagining a teacher with heavy responsibility to be both guide, co-participant, and leader for his or her students. In the Storyline case of Mr. Greg's classroom, I have described how story can promote powerful opportunities to the child as dynamic learner, searching to make sense of the world around him or her. I have discussed stories as a way of leading children into a community where each voice is important and deserving of respect and contrasted it with the homogenized terrain of textbooks and the teacher as primary source of knowledge in schools. The key to moving the center of gravity in classrooms lies with the teacher. When a teacher invites full engagement through stories from all of his or her students and shows respect for the moral teachings embedded within stories, children can begin to articulate in discussions what they care about, contrasting it with what others in the world care about. If room is made for all children, then teachers need to become full participants, too, not invisible with their voices hidden, but present and authentic in the discussion of student stories as well as in the choices of literature they offer their students. So, you may well ask, then what *is* the role of the teacher? What will the teacher do with all these dynamic, powerful ideas, feelings, and connections that story gives rise to? Where does this lead us in the classroom?

Paley sees the teacher as connection maker because children naturally want to influence one another in their work and play. Using story as a path to inquiry for students as well as self-understanding poses an epistemological dilemma for the teacher. Recall my first year of teaching students, and how serious I took my task to "teach" them. Using story calls up the question of how we know, what we know, what has been learned and what has been taught, and what is true. By opening a space for my students' stories, I came to understand how complex was the nature of teaching and learning. We will turn to this epistemological dilemma in the last part of this chapter, but first I want to explore the shift in teaching that is required to be able to fully embrace the power of story as a way of making sense of the world and for engendering habits of inquiry in our students.

We teachers can use the complexity of stories and the authenticity of our students' responses to foster their understanding, capacity for imaginative engagement, and sense-making. We see this in the story of Jason, and in the way Jo and other children construct their characters' biographies, bringing in their vision of how the world works. Both these examples are a universe away from my class that first year, when my students were isolated from both me (I was constantly reminded by my administrator to "not smile until December") and the subject matter

I loved and wanted to share. It bothered me to see how my carefully designed lesson plans actually motivated my students *out* of the learning process. What was wrong, I kept wondering. When my students helped me begin my understanding about pedagogy, leading me to question everything I had ever read or been taught about teaching, then there was really only one place for me to turn if I was ever to find the solutions: to my students themselves. By observing my students, reading their narratives, and holding dialogue—serious listening and speaking together—I began to hear many suggestive threads from which connections could be made to the content I was teaching. Later, as I worked with other teachers in other disciplines, I could see how this approach to inquiry made sense in all subjects. It wasn't the subject matter we taught, it was our students. That reversal of teaching our students as subjects now forms the basis of my pedagogy, where both my students and I are critical agents in the act of knowing together.

This is a covenant between teacher and students. "Talk to me that I may hear your questions, so that I may shape my questions for you." Teachers who forge an educative community know that there is no room for our questions until we have listened, really listened with whole mind and heart, to what students are telling us through their stories, narratives, and play. We must resist our own schooling and learn anew to locate in our students' stories their play, their actions, and their attitudes, the essence of what we need to teach. Once we see and hear anew, it is but a small step to shape our curriculum to incorporate the problems and issues our students reveal to us. Let Mr. Greg be our guide here. When he stood his ground as an adult, as authority, as Teacher, by telling the students they were not to treat the homeless in the park with such meanness, he drove their behavior and their attitudes underground. The students played the schoolgame: what the teacher doesn't know, we can go on doing or playing. When the adult point of view is dominant, students become more silent, looking instead for ways to figure out what the teachers want them to say or how to remain hidden from the teacher as a form of resistance. Either way, this is not the expansive invitation for making sense of their culture and experience that Dewey argues is vital for a democratic society or that Paley or Mr. Greg struggles with in order to foster community and connection among their students. Most definitely, what is learned, this knowledge, is quite different in substance and nature than what Jason or Jo learned. How do we know, then? And what *is* the moral power of understanding in these ways?

We can gain an important perspective in answering this question from theology. In *To Know As We Are Known,* Parker Palmer, echoing Dewey, argues against the dualism that purports that knowledge is separate from self.[13] Palmer builds upon the philosophy of John Dewey who claimed the way humans develop a mind is through social engagement with one another, sharing activities and understandings. Dewey tells us, "The conception of mind as a purely isolated possession of self is at the very antipodes of truth. The self *achieves* mind in the degree in which knowledge of things is incarnate in the life about him; the self is not a separate mind building up knowledge anew on its own account."[14] Palmer extends Dewey's argument by pointing out the risks of keeping what we know distanced from who we are as human beings, the nature that Dewey writes about that makes us social and connected.

Palmer voices strong concern about education that regards the world instrumentally, as an object to be dissected or studied or manipulated or controlled. Such a dominant way of viewing what we know, that is, striving to control and manipulate it for our own good only with no regard for consequences, may also deform us and our sense of who we are in relationship to one another and to the world we inhabit.

But for Palmer, knowledge of the world is not a neutral thing, a matter of just learning the material, receiving your "A" and going on to the next class. Nor is knowledge simply about how we use what we know for our own benefit. But such use of knowledge, motivated by curiosity, perhaps, but also control, only leads to competition and individualism, leading us to greater fragmentation and selfishness. Certainly we observe this in our society today, and in our schools, which reflect that society, this individualism and fragmentation that is present in the emphasis on grades over understanding, honor roll over cooperation, competition over community, and in the abandonment of any involvement with school whatsoever. Palmer asks if we can expect any other response when we perpetuate in our schools the attitude that one can have mastery over knowledge without thinking about how that knowledge might impact us as a person within a community and society.

However, there is another form of knowledge, claims Palmer, that emerges from compassion. This compassion turns from competition and control to seek, instead, the connection with others and, eventually the world. This is a compassion that is rooted in our kinship to one another. In this moral epistemology, we are not distanced from what we come to know nor from one another, but are instead connected by our understanding of how the world and our lives are interrelated. In such a paradigm, personal growth leads to social and intellectual development that is directly related to public life. In this view, knowing and understanding lead toward recognizing the linkages we have as humans, not just in the present, but linkages in the past and the future as well. Knowing, for Palmer, lives in compassion and love, reaching out to help us understand experience, what we read, what we discuss, and what we are living.

Education that recognizes and acts upon this way of knowing leads students into another way of being and of learning: An education of accountability, of mutuality, and of passionate involvement in learning about one's place in the world, where there is room for differences, for conflicts, and other perspectives. The self, here not the individual alone in a self-centered competitive world, is the connected self seeking to understand others, knowing that in this understanding comes understanding of self. This powerful reciprocity does not confine or manipulate or exploit the learners, nor does it encourage instrumental use of the understanding and knowledge that comes from this kinship. This is an education of authenticity and compassionate relatedness to the world that does not break it into disunited fragments, but a more coherent way of coming to see the correspondences in our world.[15] Stories are the bridge to seeing the correspondences in our world, revealing to us that knowledge is social, though it has individual dimensions.

Stories reveal and acknowledge this way of knowing ourselves or another, through our own story, another's, or when we meet a character from literature. Stories immerse us as readers in the nuances of a character's life over a period of time, whose story unfolds from the choices made. Stories help us see connections between lives and events, and offer a way to see ourselves in similar circumstances. Recall the students in Mr. Greg's classroom and the richness of their learning. Didn't they learn facts? Yes, they did. And many more facts besides because they began connecting what they lived as their characters and learned as themselves about the world's conditions. What might have been a forgettable lesson on earthquakes (do you remember your science lesson on earthquakes?) took center stage in the students' need to understand and make sense of earthquakes. Their characters' well-being depended on this understanding, since earthquakes in actuality had been experienced by many of the students themselves, and, as part of their experience, also threatened to make homeless some of their families.

Think of this leap the students made, a leap of compassionate imagination, which thrust the third graders to *imagine* the plight of those victims of an earthquake in Kobe, Japan. This was no mere lesson about earthquakes Mr. Greg taught. Students could understand through their characters' experience of being homeless (whatever the cause) that people half a world away were experiencing what their characters had to do to survive—only their plight was much worse, given the magnitude of the earthquake and loss of lives. Through compassionate imagination, Mr. Greg's students felt a kinship to those strangers in Kobe, and organized a successful canned food and relief supplies drive that was sent to Kobe within a month of the earthquake entirely through the students' efforts. We may learn facts and forget them, too, but our capacity to imagine, to see others half a world away as having needs like ours, this capacity will always be something we take with us to use throughout our life.[16]

Story is at the very heart of this ability to imagine. In this way, stories help us see who we are and push us to ask about what we believe. In this intersection our sympathies are evoked and shaped, the compassion Palmer argues for. This compassion I liken to the feeling heart of compassionate imagination, of coming to know someone different than you are without fear, a bridge across difference, which I will discuss in the next chapter.

Our society is a multicultural, pluralistic one, full of people of different cultures, ethnicities, and languages. Our public schools reflect this diversity, as well as the dominant ways society responds to minorities, that is, by trying to rend them invisible. Using stories and literature from our own cultures and the culture of others can help us see the concrete existence of a person within a contextual setting, exposing through literature the voices and language of that culture and those people.[17] I am not advocating indiscriminate use of story or literature or narrative, giving it to students and expecting them to make connections themselves, as so often happens in schools. Or worse, attaching study guide questions for each story, leaving no room for student interpretation or the invaluable discussion that can arise from different points of view. What I envision is opportunity to imagine compassionately. Nothing starves imagination more than rendering it trivial, made-up, and private so that no one hears or cares at all. Curiosity and wonder that arise out of the richness of thinking and talking about other cultures, other ways of looking at the world and living life, are evoked in our students through stories. This richness invites readers to ask questions about the lives in the story and make comparisons and connections with their own lives. Stories invite readers to enter another world where questions about life can be raised, questions that perhaps were evoked only through the narrative. And those questions emerge because through story, we are included in a specific person's struggle with dilemmas in life. The language may be different, as in the case of stories in which characters use dialects or syntax. Yet, this language can still be understood because we the readers have come to know the character and understand him through and beyond his language.

Throughout this chapter I have argued for another way teachers can help students learn authentically and spontaneously in relation to others and to the world. One way of making room for students to make connections with what they are learning is through stories, which encourage making sense of experience. In making sense of experience, students' growth is fostered. This growth is not done in isolation, but in connection with what they learn. This learning is of a particular sort: It is a learning of relatedness and correspondences, of finding out how the world works and their place in it. This learning is, as Dewey noted, a long process that should be filled with excitement—even passion—for understanding. Because learning and understanding are made social, dialogue is critically important among the participants. An important participant is the teacher herself or himself, who is as much a learner as her or his students, but helps connect what they are learning with other ideas and understanding. Constructing knowledge through dialogue is encouraged through listening and telling story and narrative, where ideas and understandings are shared publicly. Dialogue is the foundation for a democratic society and citizenship, which implies membership and shared values and concerns for the good of the total community.

Notes

1 Jerome Bruner, *Acts of Meaning*, Cambridge, Mass.: Harvard University Press, 1990, 33–65.

2 Katherine Paterson, 200.

3 John Dewey discusses dualism at great length in *Democracy and Education,* and in much of his writings because it forms the basis of an education he claimed was miseducative, not leading to the growth of the individual. For Dewey, dualism alluded to a number of things. For our purpose here I use three particular dualisms that are obstacles to understanding for our students. First: the splitting up of the subject matter itself into separate entities. Second: the way philosophy itself split up theory and practice. Third: the disconnection of the learner from the subject matter, and ultimately, claims Dewey, from one another. The barriers of dualism inhibit "free and fluent" discourse and interactions between people. xi, 70–71, 300, 343–55.

4 John Dewey, "Education as a Necessity for Life," in *Democracy and Education,* 4–13.

5 John Dewey argues here for a broad, robust notion of education that leads to educative experiences that will enable students to be in a learning community and for educators not to be taken off this task by the pressing needs of basic skills and what he calls, training. 10.

6 Here Dewey argues for an education that has immediate connections to the issues and experiences of students; that the subject matter is not isolated from their life-experiences. 11.

7 John Dewey, 4–13.

8 Valerie Polakow describes single mothers and their children living in poverty, who inhabit the margins of schools (and society). In *Lives on the Edge: Single Mothers and Their Children in the Other America* (Chicago: University of Chicago Press, 1992), Polakow presents a moving account of their stories. Her analysis of how schools treat poor children is particularly important. She argues for a pedagogy of equity and compassion, where teachers shrug off their biases and create a classroom community that respects and responds to children's experiences. Twenty-five years before Polakow wrote her book, Jonathan Kozol described the same phenomenon in Boston schools in his beautiful book, *Death at an Early Age*. Kozol tells his narrative of his year of teaching fourth grade in the Boston Public Schools. Woven among his words are the words of his students, children of poverty who already knew they were not worthwhile and experienced school as the place where their spirits were mutilated and their hearts destroyed. New York: Penguin Books, 1967.

9 Karen, Gallas. *The Languages of Learning: How Children Talk, Write, Dance, Draw, and Sing Their Understanding of the World.* New York: Teachers College Press, 1994.

10 See Paolo Freire, *Pedagogy of the Oppressed.* New York: Continuum, 1970, where he uses the metaphor of banking to describe the way traditional teachers "deposit" knowledge into students' heads so they can "withdraw" it later for a test or other assessment.

11 Vivian Paley, *The Boy Who Would Be a Helicopter.* Cambridge, Mass.: Harvard University Press, 1990, 18.

12 Ibid., 26.

13 Parker Palmer, *To Know As We Are Known: Education As a Spiritual Journey.* San Francisco: Harper, 1983.

14 John Dewey, *Democracy and Education,* 304.

15 Ibid., 16.

16 Katherine Paterson, 300.

Chapter 4

The Feeling Heart: Compassionate Imagination as an Aim and Means of an Educative Community

In the last chapter, I discussed how sense-making and connection are encouraged through the power of story. Another dimension is necessary, however, for an educative community to be forged. Civility must be present, too. Civility, like story, provides a bridge to understanding another. However, this is a particular kind of civility. This kind of civility, which I call the feeling heart, has at its center compassionate imagination that opens us to think about ourselves in relation to others, even those whom we view as unlike us. Thus, this particular civility—the feeling heart of compassionate imagination—is an important dimension of an educative community.

The Storyline topic of homelessness was a theme generated by the students, whose lack of compassionate imagination was evident in their behavior toward the homeless and in their classroom stories of "bravery" in teasing people camped out in the park. Mr. Greg, like other teachers concerned about how children treat others, did tell the students in a number of ways not to act in such cruel ways. In other classrooms, after a teacher remonstrates his students, the focus will shift back to the coursework at hand. The topic of cruelty or mean-spiritedness will be left for another incident. Telling students how to behave toward others is, after all, the constant theme in many classrooms or playgrounds.

Perhaps it is in our human nature not to question or even notice in our daily attitudes the lack of an important human quality, such as civility or a feeling heart, until it is pointed out or we are halted in our steps. Mr. Greg used Storyline to try to diminish the barriers of separation and difference in the children's attitudes that encourage a lack of compassion for another. In the Storyline about the homeless, the children created characters. Through discussion, art, and imagination, the children had to think about the lives of their homeless characters, what they might be experiencing in their daily lives and how they might be feeling. Imagining their characters' lives removes some of the obstacles that cast the homeless as the Other. When we view someone as the Other, different and separate from us, jeering and thoughtless teasing does not seem so cruel. Never thinking about how the Other might feel, we can act in thoughtless ways that cause pain without having to ever feel an obligation or responsibility for causing that pain. The role of imagination is critical in developing our ability to think about someone other than ourselves.[1] By cultivating his students' imagination, Mr. Greg hoped to evoke a sense of moral civility, of attentiveness to how another might feel or experience our actions. In so doing, Mr. Greg and his students could discuss in this context what responsibility each of us has for our own actions.

What can we as educators do to cultivate the feeling heart of compassionate imagination? First, we must define the kind of moral civility we envision as important in an educative community. To do so, I describe instances of what it looks like in the classroom. The feeling heart is conceived here as a critical attribute of an educative community that encourages the acceptance of others who are cast as different from us in both the cultural sense as well as the social sense. I am speaking here of something both deeper and richer than politeness and tolerance touted by the "politically correct." Here, differences go beyond the more obvious ones of race, ethnicity, and culture. There are differences of personality and gender and beliefs, too. Further, I will argue that a vehicle for engendering this feeling heart rests upon the imagination, which by its nature allows all students to fully engage in their process of learning, expanding their own expressions of thinking and discussing and storytelling. Because of its highly interactive and evocative nature, art presents teachers with a cornerstone to developing the bridge to understanding that opens the mind and fosters the feeling heart. Let us begin with what I mean by the civility of compassionate imagination.

The civility I speak of here is one both cognitive and emotional: an open mind and a feeling heart that fosters through imagination connections with others, especially those who are very different than we are. We get confused about civility in schools that we assume means being "nice and polite" to one another. When I was a classroom teacher, I was often struck by the ubiquitous expectation that we in our school "must treat each other courteously." Yet, daily behavior quite opposite to this expectation wore down teachers and students until the expectation was filtered out, unheard and unheeded. Many of us made efforts to bury conflict from all aspects of our classroom and school. Seeking to hide conflict, however minor, behind "politeness" only intensifies the undertow of misbehavior erupting in the halls or classrooms. While being "courteous" is a good idea, it is not what I have in mind here; in fact, later I will argue that conflict is necessary in the educative community for generating topics and themes for study, and in developing the feeling heart of compassionate imagination.

The crucial question is: How to generate open minds and feeling hearts in children? One way is through art and imagination,[2] which by their nature opens hearts and minds to seek out connections. My notion of the arts is broad and deep, encompassing literature and poetry, visual and performing, but also story and narrative from the students themselves.[3]

This Storyline provides an illustration of how civility can be fostered in the schools. In Mr. Greg's classroom, children from many walks of life, social classes, and ethnicities came together in September, a class of strangers all. Though sharing the same culture and society, students and teacher still had many bridges of difference to cross, gaps to fill. Don't we all, though? Wherever we go, we are with strangers. What happens to us is interpreted differently by each one of us. Whether we are a little boy named Le who is isolated and new to a classroom or the anthropologist Bateson sitting in a Persian garden halfway around the world, we all experience the isolation of being an outsider. So, too, do children meeting in classrooms.

Let us consider one example: Le's story. By triggering their memories of their own experiences of being new, of being an outsider, Mr. Greg acted on a number of different levels to model the feeling heart of compassionate imagination. Opening minds and hearts is the key to helping the students develop an awareness of what being new and an outsider feels like. Each child, as do we all, has keen memories of times, particularly in school, when they were the stranger, the outsider to the group. When stories start with human beings, with all the messy aspects of life, children sense that their stories, too, are important. Then there is potential for them to make meaningful connections between their life and the lives of others. Mr. Greg shares his own story of being alone in a new place, knowing no one, being confused and lost while on the schoolbus, too timid to tell the driver he did not know where his bus stop was. He invites his students to think back to their own memories of a painful experience of being alone in a new place, knowing no one.

Recall how Mr. Greg began with his own experiences, revealing his instance of vulnerability and loneliness as a child, just like Le—just like them. By doing so, he made it safe for the children to recall the times they were also scared, being alone among strangers. Situating his story in the present moment, Mr. Greg calls attention to himself, yet each and every student is a participant within his or her own memory. For a moment in time, each is new and scared (teacher, Le, students) and each feels the shift of firm ground within the safe space of their classroom, with Mr. Greg holding Big Time to ensure that all eyes are on the bunny, and not on Le. Everyone is safe to remember their fear and pain.

Mr. Greg does not run from conflict. Nor does he, as shown by this instance, reduce human life to some series of problems to be solved or fixed. No, instead he poses problems out of conflicts that arise from student experiences. Through problems such as being new, Mr. Greg invites students to explore experiences that are real and vivid to all who live in society. Activating their memories, he engages students' imagination through story. As they listen to his story, then recall their own stories, they resonate with the remembered past pain of individual experience, and imagine how Le might be feeling in the present moment. This moment is rich and many layered. One important layer is the feeling heart of compassionate imagination, reminding all participants of their interconnectedness, in spite of differences and divisions among them.

We can understand the role of imagination in cultivating the feeling heart of civility by turning to Maxine Greene. In *Releasing the Imagination,* Greene argues for the necessary role imagination plays in our cognitive and affective learning. She points to the arts, literary in particular, but all expressions of art in general, as an avenue for releasing the imagination so we can cultivate new ways of seeing and being in the world. Generating new ways of seeing and being in the world is an antidote to the mechanistic, instrumental emphasis of our society and its institutions, particularly school. Imagination has a liberating effect upon a person, and encourages an open mind and, often, an open heart. New ways of seeing and being in the world are attributes of educating for freedom, which, argues Greene, should be a goal of education. Pointing to the forces that work to undermine such an education for freedom, Greene challenges educators' acceptance of the drill and rote, disconnected information and facts posing as knowledge that often teaches students not to care about what is learned in school, that is neither questioned nor challenged by either students or teachers.[4] Where is imagination in school curriculum? Yet don't we understand the world, make it coherent, through our imagination? Where is compassion in the school curriculum? We can see how imagination and compassion are evoked in Mr Greg's class.[5]

Recall when Ashley Conder came to visit the class to show a video and talk about homeless schoolchildren. During the ensuing discussion, the children brought up the Kobe, Japan earthquake, prompting Ms. Conder to ask:

"Well, what kinds of things do you think these children might need?"

"Money" "Food" "Paper" come the responses.

Mr. Greg chimes in, "Yes, think about if you don't have any pencil or paper how you would get along in school." *Ms. Conder is nodding in agreement. She is surprised by how much the children are thinking about problems she has to deal with each day in her work with homeless children.*

"Homeless people lose things a lot," continues Ms. Conder, "because they don't have any place to store their belongings. They don't have one place."

Children are nodding and remembering how they kept misplacing their possessions because there was not one place to always keep them.

Mr. Greg looks at Tanya, "A number of our homeless characters were burnt out so they don't have any possessions at all. Annie's been burnt out, right?" Tanya says "Yes."

Sally adds, "When we went to Mexico, we saw lots of homeless people."

Dana builds on this remark, "There's probably lots of homeless people in Japan right now."

The children had made the leap from their characters' lives to the lives of others. The feeling heart, the necessity of keeping awake and alive the sense of our own experiences so as to imagine what another might feel, to what their realities might be, is fostered through imagination. Imagination, claims Greene, is the stuff that bridges differences, that allows us to imagine what might be otherwise, either in our life, in our society, or in another's experiences. The role of imagination is not to solve or fix or simply improve a situation, but to fill our seeing with light, to see what we had not seen before, and to prick us to be alert and alive. From such light, then might we be moved to act out of understanding, not defensiveness or competition. Such awareness is fundamental to being able to think about ourselves, our society, and our relationships with one another in a way that fosters understanding and connections with one another.[6] This brings us closer to the educative community that helps students prepare for associated life in democratic society. (An important direction, then, such imagining might take us is in re-visioning our place in the world as connected people.)

For Greene, democracy means community is always in the making, a process, not an end. Here the role of art is indispensable to activating the imagination of shared vision, shared connections within differences, so necessary for community. Choosing poetry and literature as her examples, Greene fills our minds with the richness of images and characters to remind us of what she is arguing for. I ask you to imagine our classrooms as cultivating both hearts and minds of our students with fairness and justice for all, in all our students' diversity, multiplicity, and complexity.

In an educative community, such growth and dynamism are actively fostered among all participants from homely situations of the participants themselves as well as the drama of national or world events. The drama of being an outsider is an internal struggle, made vivid by its very commonness. By relegating their experience as important enough to discuss and share, open channels for dialogue emerge. Perhaps later Mr. Greg might read a story to the students about being new among strangers, such as Katherine Paterson's *The Great Gilly Hopkins*, but at this point, the stage is filled with the participants in the class, sharing the stage, sharing the experience, sharing the feeling heart of civility. Differences are not diminished or homogenized. Indeed, difference is what makes the sharing of the same story interesting and lively: each has a somewhat new way of telling what they felt. Ideas about being scared, being new, are introduced. This demystifies the terror of the experience for the children as they give the names they use to describe the same thing: "shy" "nervous" "scared" "Oh, don't leave me here." These nuances of ideas foster the feeling heart of compassionate imagination.

In Japanese the word for idea is *i* which is made up of two characters from Kanji (Chinese characters in Japanese language). The first character stands for *sound*, the second character stands for *heart*. This notion that Katherine Paterson[7] pointed out in her essays is precisely what I mean by the feeling heart, where both the mind and the heart are "sounded," or in the case of the Kanji, where the idea makes a sound in the heart. Both in Hebrew and in Japanese the heart is the place where intellect and feeling are one. In the West, the heart and mind are separate functions. The civility of the feeling heart, you can see, is more in tune with the Japanese and Hebrew notions of the heart as the place where intellect and feeling are connected. Here I share a story with you about a strong memory of when I put this idea together.

The Peace Park in Hiroshima, Japan, is at the site of an industrial exposition hall that had been built with reinforced concrete. The dome shape, mangled and stark, has been left to stand as a reminder to all. On this day, thousands of schoolchildren were in Hiroshima the day the atomic bomb was dropped on the city. None escaped. Yet, unlike the rest of the city which was leveled, a wrangled mass of melted support beams and the shell of brick walls are left standing roofless in the open sky, a silent testament to what was. Following the path along the river bank leads one from the dome toward a large park, whose entrance greets one with a cenotaph, across the top of which are these words: "Rest in peace. The mistake shall not be repeated." Before the cenotaph is a plaza with two major focal points: the entrance to the museum and a large bronze statue. The statue is neither massive nor martial. Its subject evokes a reflective mode. The bronze is the representation of the moment of the flash of the atomic bomb. At its center is a teacher, a woman, who has taken as many children as possible within her shielding embrace. Her head is inclined toward the little ones, who are pressing into her skirts, some with faces looking into hers. Like the wings of the golden phoenix, her arms surround the children, drawing them in for the final embrace. The last they know will be the touch and feel of their teacher and schoolmates.

The museum entrance is to the east of the bronze statue, perhaps one hundred paces away. Inside are the shocking pictures of the horrific event, a silent reminder of the excruciating suffering of those who were not extinguished in that critical moment of explosion. Human shadows imprinted on walls or sidewalks, the remains of some of those who died instantly, are a poignant umbra of a person in the warm sun. Other photos and artifacts leave less to the imagination; the images leave no doubt as to the exquisite suffering of the survivors. You can almost hear the breaking of your heart.

Leaving the museum and entering the plaza, the arches beckon you to enter. As you look up at the words "Peace Park," they take on new meaning from your encounter in the museum. Standing at the point of entry, you see a long, still, shallow reflection pool. The eye is led to the images of sun and trees and birds which are mirrored in the pool, but at the end, as the eye follows the direction of the line, there is the mangled school building in the background. Yet around that pool are flocks of doves and pigeons, and little children feeding them with crumbs their parents have brought for this purpose. Even on this winter day, there are evergreens to offer symbolic hope of renewal. The grass and surrounding gardens are meticulously cared for, such that here in mid-winter, there is a lone azalea shyly breaking forth into white buds. It is hard to look away from the reflection pool. There are benches where one can sit in the sun, watching the children play with the birds, their images echoing in the still pool water. Through the trees I catch a glimpse of something colorful moving in the soft breeze. Curious, I walk around to the edge of the park, down a slight incline and round a bend. Before me is a shrine, the center of which is a bronze statue of a little girl with arms outstretched. A small perpetual waterfall is gurgling at the base. It is not easy to see the face of the little girl. She has been covered with handmade origami cranes, thousands of bright colored cranes placed around her neck and arms and draped all over her. Cranes are a symbol of memory, long life, and happiness in Japan. Someone has brought mikan (mandarin oranges) and placed them on a small ledge at her feet. It is New Year's in Japan, and mikan are brought to shrines as well as to homes as a symbol of good health in the coming year. Moving up the path, continuing to skirt the edges of the Peace Park, I come upon three other bronzes, all children. One is of a boy and a girl sitting on a fence ledge along the river. They, too, are covered in cranes. Another girl is sitting, reading a book. And the last is in a small clearing: two bronze statues of girls, both in poses of dancing, arms reaching to the sky, thousands of vivid origami cranes dancing with them as the breeze sways the bright birds to the unheard music of the spheres.

The Peace Park stirs the feeling heart by reminding all who see it of the fragility of life and the preciousness of children. Here, a bronze figure of a teacher shields and bends toward the frightened little ones to protect with all she has, her body. As one gazes at the figures, there stirs in the heart a resounding affirmation of the connectedness of all human beings—that what we do unto others affects us in return. That perhaps, even, there is no difference in our hearts at all—we are all one people. Perhaps this is what we are to learn in our existence together, or continue to pay unthinkable costs in human suffering.

The lesson I learned during my visit to the Peace Park was the power of an experience so unimaginable, so horrific that no one in their right mind could stand to comprehend such an event. Our inclination, as humans, might be to look away, to resist the urge to feel—for how can anyone truly want to imagine or feel such pain. Whoever designed the Peace Park, though, deeply understood the mediating power of art to forge connections, to create a space large enough for another's thoughts, dreams, ideas, and heart. The mediating power of art is crucial, I believe, to bring us into the lives of others so that we might experience our own life as connected to others. As I walked among strangers all that day in the Peace Park, each of us brought our own story and experiences with us. In gazing at the bronze children, however, even our being strangers could not avert our glances. I do not know the names of those whose eyes mine met, nor do I know what languages would express what they saw, but in that place under blue sky, so many, many years after the bomb fell, we all experienced a kind of mutuality, and for me, the feeling heart stirred with that shared meaning. I experienced an encounter with compassionate imagination that would move my own growth as a person.

Our task as educators is to help each child develop the feeling heart of compassionate imagination. Recall the Kanji for the concept of *idea*: one character stands for *sound,* the other for *heart.* I think we must help our students listen to the sound of their feeling heart. Evoking the power of the imagination, the feeling heart takes us away from the more traditional approaches to civility found in schools. Art and imagination demand other, different, new ways of listening within ourselves what ideas are evoked by art. In so listening, art and imagination can summon the feeling heart in our students. And as we evoke the feeling heart, we might experience the mutuality that connects us in the classroom; the experiences of many could be a harbinger for the mutuality of being in the world together.

Mary Catherine Bateson persuasively argues for developing new ways of seeing, and for celebrating our increasing plurality so that we teachers and students might better develop insight through conflict and difference. In *Peripheral Vision: Learning Along the Way*, Bateson embraces the diversity in our society claiming that through this diversity (with its attendant conflict, contradiction, and desperateness) we are allowed to see in ways not possible when we cling to homogeneity and uniformity.[8] Our natural inclination is to turn away from difference with an unwillingness to contemplate other ways of being in the world across diverse cultures. Yet, claims Bateson, when we turn away from such offerings we deny more than the ambiguity we reject, we are turning away from learning and turning away we fail. We fail at compassion. We fail at empathy. We fail in our imagination.

A society that fails at compassion that is combined with resistance to new learning threatens us all. We need little imagination to glimpse the consequences. Schools have erupted as sites of violence and carnage. Padukah, KY; Jonesboro, AR; Springfield, OR; Littleton, CO; and others all stare out at us in the newspaper headlines. Our students are telling us that school isn't working for them. Our collective educational response is more control, putting metal detectors in schools, tighter rules, and more. Passing test scores and good grades alone do little to ensure that we are cultivating sound in both heart and mind, and that the stranger (or our classmates) among us will not lash out against any of us.

How do we want to prepare our children for the future? This stasis is the antithesis of what educative community fosters. It is in schools where we have the students as young strangers that we can sow the seeds of the feeling heart of compassionate imagination as they learn about themselves and the world. In the educative community, students are invited to participate in understanding and making sense of the world together. All belong and are respected members of an educative community that pays attention to one another.

One of the ways that school can become a place where the feeling heart is cultivated is to acknowledge the lessons brought to us by the students themselves. Mr. Greg took homelessness as a topic because this is what the children were bringing into the classroom. Such a generative topic offered the conflict and tensions between public and private needs and obligations we have as members in a democratic society. By weaving the connection of the classroom responses to the homeless a few blocks away in the park with the children's actions towards one another (and their characters) in the class, and then presenting an ever greater exposure to the community and the public world, Mr. Greg encouraged his students to think about the plight of the homeless and then link it with what it must feel like to be homeless. The idea of homelessness became a sound in their hearts as they thought more each day about their homeless characters and what they endured.

I remember sitting by Sal and hearing about his character Robert's wish to die. The tone of the entire class was immediately subdued. They took seriously Robert's desire to end it all. They seemed to grasp what it might mean to have so little hope that there was no other option. Only a couple of the children voiced hushed objections to Robert's declaration. Sal turned to me and we said nothing, just locked our eyes for that moment. Such encounters with another person's desire—even though everyone knew on a cognitive level that Robert was "only a character"—stretches our imaginations and helps us to reach out toward people whose lives differ from our own. The gaze Sal and I exchanged was one of mutual understanding and echoed of other gazes I shared in the Peace Park, the feeling heart.

Art, in this case the paper representation of the character Robert's face, became a vehicle to unlock some of the beliefs the students carried within them about the homeless, but now it was with a weakened sense of stereotyping that had before prompted the participation in jeering and heckling the homeless. This stated belief, that Robert really wants to die, has a power that students can believe. Robert has an identity and a social standing among the students. He is, in short, a member, no longer a stranger. All these homeless characters and their stories represent the students' ideas. During the Storyline, a communal, compassionate imagination has stirred, as students developed their characters' stories and as they thought of new associations.

The feeling heart can stir our compassionate imagination for another. In so doing we become open to the connections between ourselves and others. Experiencing the power of the shared self can enhance our understanding of human values in a pluralistic world, sustain the civility of our human society, and increase our appreciation for and involvement with one another. In this chapter, I have discussed the importance of imagination for the feeling heart to take root. To paraphrase Maxine Greene we can teach through the imagination as the window to bring us face to face with different viewpoints, perspectives, interests and ways of living.[9] "Here we are" say our students by their very presence as they come into our classrooms each fall. Strangers at our door, our students come to us from diverse and plural associations. How do we make this a community of known people? How do we foster respect and recognition without the fear of being exposed to the reality of the lives of others who are in different circumstances from our own? As Plato wrote: What is honored in a country will be cultivated there. What do we honor in our country? In the next chapter, I discuss the crucial issue of membership in community, as a sense of belonging.

Notes

1 In *Love's Knowledge*, Martha Nussbaum writes about the moral imagination engendered through literature. Through literature with the particular lives of characters, we can come to wrestle with ethical and moral issues vicariously. New York: Oxford University Press, 1990, 391.

2 Maxine Greene, *Releasing the Imagination: Essays on Education, the Arts, and Social Change.* San Francisco: Jossey-Bass, 1995.

3 Northrup Frye writes in *The Educated Imagination* that it is our imagination that propels our entire social life together, making it possible to combine what we feel and how we think in ways we can be understood and others can understand us. Bloomington: Indiana University Press, 1964, 135.

4 For further discussion of the idea of expressive knowing and the centrality of aesthetic awareness through life, see John Dewey, *Art and Experience*, New York: Perigree Books, 1934, especially chapter 4; Kieran Egan, *Primary Understanding*, New York: Routledge, 1988. Egan's argument is pertinent in our discussion when he claims that educational foundations are in essence poetic. See especially chapter 5; Northrup Frye, *The Educated Imagination*, especially chapter 4, where he argues for the teaching of literature to foster imaginative growth. For another perspective linking art and identity, see "On Civil Society and Social Identity" by Ivan Karp, pp. 19–33, and Edmund Barry Gaither's chapter 2, "Hey! That's Mine: Thoughts on Pluralism and American Museums", pp. 56–64. *Museums and Communities: The Politics of Public Culture,* ed. Ivan Karp, Christine Mullen Dreamer, and Steven D. Lavine. Washington D.C.: Smithsonian Institution Press, 1992.

5 Maxine Greene, 2.

6 Ibid., 28.

7 Katherine Paterson.

8 Mary Catherine Bateson, *Peripheral Vision: Learning Along the Way.* New York: HarperCollins, 1994.

9 Maxine Greene, 31.

Chapter 5

Belonging and the Terror of It All: A Sense of Belonging as an Aim and Means of an Educative Community

The educative elements discussed in this book—trust, communal ways of understanding, and the feeling heart of compassionate imagination—offer teachers opportunities to strengthen their students' personal, social, and intellectual capacities to engage in public life. This work has discussed how these elements are constituted through participation, problem-posing, dialogic relations, and compassionate imagination. It has illustrated how the skills of reading, writing, and thinking are enriched and enhanced through these constitutive acts. And it is through these acts teachers acknowledge and affirm their students as recognized and respected persons. But are these elements enough to guarantee an educative community? Only by recognizing each and every member of the classroom can we offer the space so an educative community can be forged. This is easier said than done.

Students come to us from many diverse communities; as teachers, we cannot or do not choose who our students will be. We open the door and they say "Here we are!" It is in the nature of our public school system that if children come to school, they are taken in: a place must be made for them. For the thirty or so children, all strangers to *us*, how do we forge a community? How will we all connect to one another, these strangers at our door? Just because students are in a room together does not ensure there is a community. To be included in the class is more than just having a desk, just showing up every day.

In this chapter, I argue that a sense of belonging is an outgrowth of membership in a classroom community where the elements of trust, communal ways of understanding, and the feeling heart of compassionate imagination are alive and in place. Recognized and respected, we can present our authentic selves to each other through dialogue and our interactions. Respect and recognition of difference, even with no resolution, offer a useful tension among members. This potentially generative tension can sustain ambiguity, conflict, and complexity that arise between people who are unlike one another. It can enlarge and enrich our vision of the world while at the same time challenging it. Under such conditions we constantly reconsider our way of being and thinking and relating. Creative tension, I argue, supports and fosters growth and possible transformation.

If we can maintain this tension, we can present our authentic selves to one another, develop a sense of belonging, and forge bonds of relationships and connections. In turn, a sense of belonging replaces our habits of defensiveness and fear with habits of compassionate imagination, allowing us to engage with those unlike ourselves in open exchange. This growth fosters our capacity to engage in public life with people who believe or act or see the world differently than we do. In a classroom, when there is a sense of belonging among participants, an educative community can make the space for difference, conflict, ambiguity.

But terror is present in this recurring act of forging such a community. When we must learn how to envision each other, when we learn to trust ourselves and each other, we open ourselves to the *pain* of discovery, of growth and possible transformation. It seems that by the time we may begin to figure out with our class just how to forge this community, the year is over and we must begin anew. To continually create and re-create community with our students day by day as well as year after year is not only a tremendous amount of work for both teachers and students, but it's also a scary one, for it means we are constantly caught in the current of new ways of being in community. We can never assume we know how to forge an educative community. Each new group demands we must learn new ways of listening and speaking and connecting with them. In part, this is what gives teaching its joyous components—and its painful ones, because we are challenged by our students' beliefs and attitudes, perhaps even more than they are with ours.

In this chapter, I will discuss the necessity of membership for the fostering of a sense of belonging. From there I will explore my vision of an educative community, and how it might be forged with the full membership of all participants. The last section will address the terrors both teachers and students must grapple with if an educative community is to function. I begin with membership.

Recall the story of Le. He was the new boy in class, arriving on my first day with the third graders and Mr. Greg. By evoking memories of their own first day experiences, and sharing his own story, too, the teacher brought Le from outsider to one of the community. He was no stranger, this person who, like they (and we) had been once, did not know anyone, and was alone. I am reminded of my own struggles to be recognized and to feel as if I belonged. If Le's history with the class was just beginning, it was certainly built on the other children's understanding that they, too, had once been new students standing among strangers. Their memories had been so close to the surface it took only a question from the teacher to bring them forward. Le couldn't be so different if he were going through what they had. Here was the beginning of membership in this classroom community, with promise that he could be one of them. Once they saw Le as part of the group, the shared experience, shared meanings, and shared understandings could develop even with the difference of his culture, language, and ways of being in the world. Being admitted as a member of the classroom community did not guarantee Le would feel a sense of belonging, but it was the first step toward it. So let us turn to what it means to become a member of a community.

An important question is who decides what it means to become a member? What constitutes community and how might it be cultivated is decided among the participants, students and teacher. And what about membership within the community for those who come from diverse ethnic, cultural, and racial backgrounds? There is no easy way to get to community of any sort, much less an educative one.

The pluralism of our society creates tension between what is good for one or some and what is good for all. Such is the character of a democratic society, always dynamic and striving to locate some balance out of the competing tensions between individuals and the common good. However, here are some things we can keep in mind. For instance, in *Spheres of Justice* Michael Walzer suggests what things transform congeries into communities. The most central aspects of transforming congeries into communities are membership and recognition of all members so they may exchange the social goods Walzer describes. Membership can foster a sense of belonging, but a sense of belonging is not automatically fostered through membership.

Membership is a necessary step toward forging an educative community, but even when we have membership we do not necessarily have a community. Too often we construct a simplistic ideal of community in which differences are flattened as the price of membership. Yes, before we can have a sense of belonging, we have to have membership first. Walzer explains that we distribute membership to one another and, as such, membership is a good amongst a group of persons. By this I take him to mean that membership itself is a social good, something we distribute (or not) according to what we choose to do. The role of a teacher, I contend, is to foster the conditions for membership in the classroom. This is an important step.

Walzer actually gives three principles that underlie his theory of distributive justice, in other words, who gets what and how they get it. He says, and we will substitute the notion of classroom community rather than his term describing political community here:

> Every [classroom] determines its needs as a community and pays attention to those needs;
> Distribution of goods to members pays attention to member needs accordingly;
> All members are equal and are recognized by other members as such.

It is this last principle that I want to emphasize in this chapter. To be a member means you have been taken in, accepted into the group. The community is a good and is distributed by accepting people into itself.[1] Membership, then, consists in belonging to a group where social goods are distributed and exchanged amongst the members and, as such, is itself a primary social good. Michael Walzer describes a vision of a society where all people are accorded equality simply because they are human and deserve recognition, a society where domination cannot force a privileged distribution of the social goods of society.[2] Walzer argues that recognition is requisite for membership in society where exchanges are part of relationships. Spheres, for Walzer, are domains of human society where goods are exchanged, divided, and shared.[3] Our standing as members of society, as members of communities, is relational and contingent upon recognition of one another.

Such a powerful image is made more so by the political, social, economic, and racial divisions that separate us in our culture and society. As a teacher I was endlessly having to mediate between students who were angry or felt rejected about being left out. Though I frequently had students work together in projects, they carried into their tasks the same issues experienced in the halls or on the playground. "So and so does this a different way, so how can he be in our group?" and "She doesn't know how to work *our* way," come from a similar source about who belongs and who does not. How do we know who to take in? How do we decide? On what grounds? These questions raise the spectre of complexity with its attendant characteristics of ambiguity, conflict, and difference that challenge us to grow in our capacity to consider other ways of being in the world.

Ambiguity, conflict, and difference can be contained in many ways by communities. I am not advocating for a community where all must be like each other, or where there is no room for dissent as the price for belonging. Lois Lowry's *The Giver* is a children's book about a society that has successfully stamped out all difference, all conflict, all selfishness, and all individuality for the sake of "community" and peace, where all are guaranteed a place in society.[4] The flattened, colorless landscape is matched by the rigid roles people are assigned and the passionless way they live out their lives. No room for imagination is given child or adult because all must be committed to the peace of the community, to togetherness. While extreme, nevertheless, *The Giver* provides us with strong lessons of what we give up by closing down our individuality and our differences, the very diversity that I think enlivens our society and culture. The price is high, in some communities, for admittance. To give up one's integrity and individuality in order to ensure belonging to a community is a terror. And clearly, this community would fit neither with Walzer's notion of distributive justice nor with my notion of an educative community.

Nor am I advocating for a community where membership assures members that they are safe from all who disagree or are different. The security that might be bought from this conformity leaves no room for compassionate imagination or other people's stories or trust that you will be recognized and respected for who you are. To contain ambiguity by constricting all forms of difference and conflict closes us from the very growth Dewey said was so vital to the existence of our democracy. While it may make life seem calm and secure, the cost is that we maintain barriers to all those whom we deem unlike us. We see this in some fundamentalist religions and cults, existing by building metaphorical (and sometimes real) walls between their community and everyone else. We can see how this leads to fractious and uneasy relations, and certainly instills habits of heart and mind that make us suspicious and fearful of all who are different.

To get clear about the character of community that would be educative (and coincidentally democratic), let us ask what would be the educative point of membership. To answer this we must look at another question: What is the goal or purpose of education? The answer has been implied throughout this thesis: The goal of education is to connect personal growth to social and public life. Note that personal growth encompasses all aspects of a person: the social, the intellectual, the personal, and, yes, even the spiritual. As sages throughout human history have observed, we humans are more alike than different, but it is difference that too often motivates us to act. In forging an educative community, we must pay close attention to honoring both what is similar and what is different among us. In the act of forging shared meanings and understandings, we create our own good: the community itself, local and particular. While we may know what our goal is, in this case, to foster community and a sense of belonging in our classrooms, it also means that there is no set procedure or rules to follow algorithmically. Each of us has to develop within ourselves the alertness and vision to imagine how we will foster community in our classrooms. Yet, though we have no rules to follow, our imagination and vision can be our guides as we work with our students. I assure you, once you have been part of an educative community, you will not forget it. Living in an educative community, even for one term, simply "ruins" you; that is, you will always know when it is absent.

The significant good, the potential for equality and recognition is cultivated by our openness to bring others into our group. Acts of trusting, the act of moral imagination, and acts of understanding others' stories build community. Without membership in a community built on such acts, our children become disconnected from each other, and from us. This is why we need a sense of belonging to the educative community. But membership alone does not ensure an *educative* community. Membership, argues Walzer, is built upon shared culture and understanding.[5] The educative community is dynamic and mutable, but with membership, participants can build on the foundation of their shared beliefs, shared meanings, and shared understandings to foster a sense of belonging. Only when there is a sense of belonging with all its attendant attributes among participants do we know that the educative community is present.

Let us continue with the analogy between the political community and the school classroom. Both require common meanings. In such places as schools we as members can assert ourselves and create our sense of history and meanings; think of yearbooks, of particular school activities, of even the ritual closing of school at the end of the year. In spite of such events as above, there is underlying them all a sense of admission and exclusion in groups within the school, all of which is supposed to add up to an entire school community. This is the basis of the common life together, where a community has shared meanings and a history of understandings and associations with each other. In other words, within our community we are historically connected one to another in varying degrees of strength. In our classrooms, our history begins each year as soon as our students arrive. We cannot wait to smile until December, as the old teacher adage warns us, so that we can "keep the lid on." So much is at stake from the first moment we meet and greet our students.

If we accept the analogy of the classroom as a site where members divide, exchange, and share their social goods among themselves, we can see that the notion of admission and exclusion is crucial.[6] Students come to school and are "taken in." A teacher does not choose her pupils, but must admit them to his or her class. If the teacher and students accept the new student, membership and the potential for commonalty and shared meanings begin. However, our public schools, among other institutions, argues Walzer, are of little use unless they are inhabited by men and women (and girls and boys) who feel safe and secure within them.[7] If this is so, then this is why we must go beyond membership and foster a sense of belonging, which constitutes an educative community. This brings us to our next section where we will explore the reasons why we need to foster a sense of belonging after we have gotten to the stage of full membership for all. What do we gain through membership and fostering a sense of belonging?

Only through membership in a society can people hope to create, exchange, and obtain goods, the social goods necessary for a good life. When members have the hope that each can share in the social goods of communal life, goods such as recognition, security, agency, then belonging to a community means the opportunity to receive those goods. It would follow that if a classroom is a place where we might be members, then what are the social goods that might be exchanged if within that domain existed an educative community? We have much at stake in the answer. In the last part of our twentieth century, schools have reeled from catastrophic and tragic actions by students who feel unrecognized and hopeless about receiving any goods of membership because they do not believe they are part of the school community generally. This notion of a sense of belonging is a serious one for us as teachers. Some might say our lives depend on it. Utilizing Walzer's theory of distributive justice, I see four social goods that might be exchanged in an educative community and that identify growth necessary to entering into public life.

The first good distributed in an educative community is the *capacity to tolerate conflict*. What kind of conflict does an educative community require? Not conflict that is combative, destructive, and diminishing to any of us. Such forms of conflict need to be eliminated from our life together, particularly in our classrooms. Education requires a form of conflict that does not seek to dominate or destroy difference. Rather, it can sustain disagreement and difference and hold it in creative tension. Conflict held in creative tension does not seek to remake others into our likeness, but instead creates space so we can have our connectedness revealed without losing our sense of integrity and identity. The educative community becomes a place, then, where different voices and ideas are listened to and encouraged, and where the potential for shared understandings will be increased. Through genuine dialogue, understandings are fostered and our fear of others unlike us and who hold another way of thinking about the world is diluted and diminished, making way for a sense of belonging amongst members.

The second social good of an educative community is *tolerance for difference*. Difference makes life complicated, especially in schools and in our classrooms. What may be important to one is ignored by another. In an educative community each person is respected and recognized as subjects (not objects) who bring his and her lived experiences into the community. (Indeed, these lived experiences are invited and welcomed.) The context allows for people to be different, unlike in *The Giver* where no one was allowed any deviation from the norm or else they would be "released," and never heard or seen again. But in an educative community, difference is not threatening to one's sense of self. Compassionate imagination of the feeling heart provides an opening to understandings between the participants. Each can hear the other's story, perhaps, as Neusner says, finding his own story in it and locating shared beliefs.

Tolerance of ambiguity is the third social good exchanged within an educative community. Ambiguity is brought on by the complexity of being with others who are unlike ourselves, who bring stories that challenge ours. Ambiguity is the direct outgrowth of conflict and difference, all wrapped up in confusion and discomfort. The certainty that provides us with some foundation about the world is thrown up in the air, beyond our reach. In an educative community, this uncertainty is named and recognized. But there is a perception that we are all in this together and that any differences are soluble. This does not mean there is a solution for every problem; that is a lie. Honest, authentic relationships generate naturally degrees of ambiguity. Because of a high level of trust among the participants, diverse perspectives give rise to shared meanings. Space is given to think about their own interpretations of what is heard, experienced, and felt. Trust allows us to listen to each other, and still have the freedom to imagine our own way of seeing.

And the most important social good achieved is *a sense of belonging* itself, which is created and revived through genuine dialogue out of respect and recognition. Through a sense of belonging, we can be authentic in our relations with others, and tolerate situations where conflict exists and resolution does not.[8] We can engage with others in dialogue built upon respect and recognition. Awareness develops through multiple interactions that people see in more than one way. Difference is tolerated because there is no loss of self, no sense that we are diminished by diversity.

The path toward the social goods of an educative community is rough, uneven, and without a map to guide us. Why is it so difficult for us, teachers and students, to forge an educative community? I think we have to think about some of the obstacles that keep us from trusting, from civility, and communal ways of understanding, each of which cultivates an educative community. Obstacles that prevent us from constituting an educative community within our classrooms often elicit fear and resistance from us as teachers. I call these teacher terrors.

First of all, I want to say that it takes courage to teach. As teachers, we stand in the public place of school and must give our authentic selves over to the task of connecting with our students and the subject matter. We who have been in classrooms as students, then as teachers, know there are myriad roadblocks obscuring the vision I share with you of an educative community. Let me be explicit about some of these obstacles that I see as responses to the pain of discovery, of growth, and of transformation—what I call the terror. As a teacher I was concerned about "keeping the lid on" as my first principal frequently reminded us in the daily bulletin. As with most first-year teachers, I felt vulnerable, overworked, inadequate to the task of teaching my students, getting to know them, and being responsible to my colleagues, school, and district. So I kept "the lid on" and maintained control over my classes by subtle (and not so subtle) reminders of my authority as The Teacher. In so doing, I could see how there was security in knowing the rules, for both me and my students. I had the security as an authority of knowledge and as a figure of authority in my standing as a teacher. And there was another type of security I discovered, too. And that was the security of *thinking* that I was in control and viewed as someone who had some power. In keeping power and control as foundational to my teaching, I successfully kept my students at a distance. Educating was something I did to my students, not something we experienced together, as my students and I came to do later. Each of us at some point in our teaching career, I am convinced, comes to realize that when we get up in front of a class it is our students who give us leave to teach them. I did not understand this back then.

The terror I felt as a first-year teacher I still carry with me even after my many years in the classroom. I think I will always feel that twinge of fear each time I teach because at the heart of it, teaching is a vulnerable act, the intersection between private person and public person. I stand in the public place (before my students) and I must be open, authentic, wholly present. And I cannot teach without their presence. In order to teach, I need my students. I must always strive for connection and never lose my courage (and hope) that I can reach them, despite difficulties and struggles that present themselves with new students each year. And also I must remember that for my students there are terrors as well.

Remember Mr. Gradgrind? Sissy's description of a horse was deemed inadequate by the expert teacher. His response to her attempt to answer his question left her wide open for humiliation and defeat. She had no other resource except to retreat in silence and hope he never notices her again. Students also feel the terror when a teacher asks them to engage with and to think critically about a topic. What if thinking challenged them? To take a risk leaves a person open to hurt. It might change them. That would mean they would have to not only invest themselves but open themselves up for judgment and evaluation and possible rejection. Much safer to know the rules and keep at a distance, choosing to follow the rules or not to—with little or no involvement of responsibility and obligation either to one another or with me as their teacher. Students have learned it is easier to keep distance from the teacher and learning when both are objectified. They seem to seek the feeling of safety that distance affords. Yet this is a trap: to keep distance from others and from learning is isolating. The paradox was that my students constantly struggled with disconnection: from one another, from family, from school, and from their teachers. When I imposed learning upon them, they responded with well-practiced resistance, as well they should have. Here I was taking my classes of young adolescents and fostering even more disconnection by the control I exercised over them through my teaching. Resistance to more imposition came in the form of note passing, whispering, sudden and disruptive noises, interruptions, and, my all-time favorite, pretending not to "get it." If you don't "get it" how can you be held responsible? Resistance to anything that might deepen understanding took (and for many students still takes) a great deal of effort. But it's an effort that is worth it if the security of distance is maintained.

So there are teacher terrors and there are student terrors that are barriers to forming an educative community. Some feel more secure when our roles are defined and rules are imposed. Again, the paradox is that such security is itself precarious and superficial. In our diverse society, we do not usually know all the rules or cultural codes of others. That is what we must learn to decipher so we might hold dialogue with those unlike ourselves, and this should be a benefit from being in a public school in our democratic society. Yes, we may briefly feel better about keeping learning objectified and one another at arm's length, but these are the very walls we must scale to be engaged in learning, to hear one another's story, to learn to be in community together. What is it behind the barrier that prevents us from forging an educative community? Is it more than convenience to control students, dispensing knowledge into their "empty vessels" and insisting that they please not bring their selfhood to school? What *are* we keeping the lid on for? We open ourselves to being known as well as coming to know others. When a teacher is open and respectful, this invites students into relations where obligation and connection bring responsibility. Furthermore, it opens the teacher to having to be authentic and wholly present with her students, which means we must be aware of the condition of our hearts and souls, as well as our minds. Being open to one another dissolves the distance between us. Having to interact with others, to "become" which is the result of this interaction, can lead us to be changed and conscious of our commonalties as humans. Our very human relationships are fraught with shards of ambiguity and conflict, swirling about in our own complexity. All these elements are present when we try to connect with another person. In school, "keeping the lid on" is a way of telling teachers to keep distance between us and our students, and between students themselves.

We have exchanged the old terrors for a new one: *the threat of transformation*. Within such relationship is the potential of being challenged and changed by learning together and being with others in community. That means we invite ambiguity and the complexity of different ways of seeing the world right into our room, and by this invitation we become vulnerable to knowledge and experience that may influence us to see in new ways. When we resist, is it because we are afraid of being altered? Through genuine dialogue of mutual respect and reciprocity, the distance between students and teachers is reduced, setting the stage for shared understandings, beliefs, and meanings. With such relations, each of us becomes obligated to respect and recognize one another. Connections are forged, and, even with our differences, we are linked by shared experiences, understandings, and our socially constructed meanings. A complex web of interactions develops and makes transformation possible. I think this is a scary prospect for many people who see any or all change as giving up something within themselves. For some it might be having to let go of the security of a belief about a group of people, or having a worldview challenged by new perspectives, or having the experience of being moved by another person's story. In such small acts, the seeds of transformation are cultivated. Transformation thrusts us into terra incognita, and I don't know anyone who relishes the feeling of being lost in an uncharted landscape. Where is some security for us, some sense of rootedness? If we begin to open ourselves to one another through trust, story, and the feeling heart we also open a Pandora's box, out of which flies ambiguity, difference, conflict, complexity, and the terror of it all.

In the educative community envisioned here, problems are considered social, if not always soluble, but not personal failings or insurmountable facts to learn.[9] We saw how the children in Mr. Gregs classroom developed an awareness of the plight of the homeless. In this process, their beliefs and attitudes were shifted toward a more compassionate stance toward the homeless. The problem of homelessness is a crucial issue in our society, one that the children (at least right now) cannot solve. At the same time, their own transformation in thinking about the homeless is within their grasp. I believe they learned more about homelessness through their Storyline characters' struggles with living on the street than any other lesson Mr. Greg and I might have offered. And like all teachers, Mr. Greg will not know how deeply the children did come to understand or if every child experienced a transformation at some level or, that one day, one of these third graders will distinguish herself or himself as someone who does indeed make a contribution to our society that erases homelessness. We don't know. All that matters is that all of us remain wholly present to our students and teach them as if our very lives depended on it.

Working with students by emphasizing that problems are social and soluble helps them to consider other ways of being in the world; it widens their horizons to learn what it means to be participants in public life. School, and in particular, a classroom can provide meaningful contexts to students so the skills and critical inquiry connect them with what they understand and with what they learn and with the possibility of their own transformation. Our efforts as educators should be to identify and make sense of that which brings us into community so those experiences will foster growth of intelligence, of social understanding, of personal reflection, and of a sense of belonging in our students.

The classroom can be a special place, a meeting place, where people who are different encounter one another. The quality of the dialogue and relations is enhanced when people in the classroom can feel recognized and respected for who they are and what they bring to the class. The tension is ever present, though, as our classrooms become meeting places of children from diverse communities in our society. The classroom is not an apolitical space: the inhabitants bring in their beliefs, experiences, fears, and expectations perceived through the lenses of their own cultures, communities, and demons.

School is a meeting place for people who happen to be students or teachers, who are placed together for a year or more. And it is the obligation of teachers to help students connect with one another and themselves, not the other way around, that is, not the obligation of students to connect with their teachers and one another. For there to be a sense of belonging in a community there has to be shared meanings, shared understandings, shared experiences. How do we share when we are so unlike each other? A teacher has to be alert to and constantly seek to identify and develop those shared events and understandings that cohere a group. This means we need to make space for a plurality of understandings. Each brings a different notion with him or her about what it means to belong to a community. Again, here is where the compassionate imagination is needed to allow for those differences and conflicts that naturally will arise amongst people generally, but where plurality is present, most certainly.

We bring in our different stories to the classroom and by doing so we track in the political forces of our society. But we do not need to reproduce or perpetuate those forces, often inequitable and dominating, that many of us, students and teachers, have experienced in society. Our classroom can instill a different approach, a different procedure, a sense of belonging. It can be a place where we learn about being in relation to one another and what it means to be a member of a community made up of those who are/were strangers. In our democratic society, we want our children to be able to engage in public life together, able to tolerate the ambiguity that comes from many different perspectives on what it means to live in society. What I mean is that differences, conflicts, ambiguity all can be tolerated because *of* belonging to an educative community, where the terror of disconnection and exclusion is checked.

Recall Peter's comment to Mr. Greg about the classroom having an ugly teacher. His attempt to distance himself from participating in the class discussion was neutralized by Mr. Greg's calm, respectful response. "Do you really want to base your description on something others may not agree with?" Disconnection, deeply ingrained in us, is often at the root of children's behaviors. Mr. Greg therefore sought to give Peter enough opportunity to connect again, knowing that old habits of mind take a long time to change. Disconnection was at the root between the children and the homeless people in the park. The common "enemy" gave the children a common object to exclude and at the same time emphasize their own inclusion. If we all can agree on who the outsider, the different one, is, then we are connected in our agreement. Why did they do this? Because children, like adults, yearn for connection and seek it out, even in this weakened and, I think, distorted way of finding a scapegoat in common. Teachers can guide students into more robust, moral connections that lead to understanding in imaginative, compassionate ways, but first the children must be listened to. As with the element of trust, we cannot tell and direct our students into robust, hearty connections. In other words, we cannot get to this directly, but through an educative community, healthy connections between members can be fostered, and new ways of seeing the world explored.

Through their characters' stories, the children gave clues to their more subterranean beliefs about homeless people, but also about their own feelings and fears about belonging and exclusion, about their own desires to connect with others. The need to belong and be connected is very deep in us; we want to belong so much, yet withhold this "good" from others, especially those we see as different. The children grouped the characters according to particular attributes, making assumptions about who was friends with whom.

Recall, Mr. Greg asks if any of the homeless characters know each other. Even though Tingtong's and Redhead's creators are absent that day, a number of children say they are sure these two know each other.

What makes you think they know each other?" asks Mr. Greg.

"Because they both look weird, that's why." Though Sal is the one who says this, other children are nodding in agreement.

"Weirdness" is a reason for being friends. "Weirdness" is a reason you do not get to choose your friends. No one in this class wants to be weird, because that would mean they could only be with other weird kids. Mr. Greg, always on the alert on the playground or in class to bring to the surface issues that loom large in the children's lives, uses what the children tell him as a springboard for helping them reflect on their beliefs. For this teacher, the minds of his students are paramount. That means he is alert to those experiences that will develop the minds of his students. And the mind, as opposed to the brain, encompasses the heart, the spirit of being human in thought and deed. Mr. Greg knows that there is more to learning than reading and writing. Understanding and connection to one's own life are features of learning that foster growth and lead to sense-making.

But our society places pressure upon schools to keep to the business of "educating," that is, teaching basic skills to students.[10] In *Releasing the Imagination,* Maxine Greene writes about notions of community and school.[11] She reminds us that community cannot be taken for granted or a name conferred, as when we put a group of people together and then say, "There. Now you are a community." Instead like democracy, community is constituted by all of us occupying a space together. Within our classroom we can invite our students to discover and appreciate that which they hold in common. Community is shared experience and our relationships to one another. Our relationships are imagined, then developed and fostered by persons alert to this dimension of community. The compassionate imagination of the feeling heart is necessary here.

In her book *Schooling Homeless Children*, Sharon Quint asks her reader to imagine what we do in school as the life of our ordinary interactions and problems we experience in life.[12] She asks us to imagine teachers who guide students in developing skills to live in a civil society. She presents images of possibilities when she paints a picture of a school where learning includes coming to know and understand one another, ourselves, as well as the prescribed curriculum—all are woven as part of each other, not kept separate. Quint asks us to imagine a school where priority for helping children fulfill their capacities as beings of the world is honored.[13] It seems such a simple idea that a child's education can truly begin when a sense of belonging is experienced in an educative community, yet judging by the school reform literature it is apparently not a broadly obvious notion.[14]

I have identified elements of an educative community, but there are no guidelines or rules to follow to get there. This is why it is so difficult for us to imagine and envision. Yet we know that we have an obligation and responsibility to those we teach to foster growth. Genuine education helps us grow: intellectually, socially, personally. And it is this growth that will assist us in becoming present to ourselves and a participant in public life of our democracy. Because of a sense of belonging, our educative community can welcome diversity and conflict, tolerate ambiguity, and embrace the paradox within an ethos of trust, narrative ways of knowing and civility. When viewed in this way, education becomes robust and broad, connecting people together so they come to live their common humanity. Education here is meant to unite, not divide people. The educative community should be our goal in schooling, taking in the art of pedagogy—learning, knowing, and teaching—as a way to weave connections with each other *without the disconnection of giving up who we are or what we bring with us from our selves.*

Within an educative community we forge bonds of intimacy, but we do not stop there. We want more than a safe place where we can trust and respect within the civility of the school and classroom. By themselves, trust and civility are not enough to sustain the educative community I envision. We have to foster a sense of connection and belongingness with others. These elements of trust, narrative ways of knowing, and civility are crucial to an educative community and, when there is a sense of belonging, mutually sustainable. And when this happens in an educative community, learning to know leads to knowing to learn, moving to product through process and back again. Learning and knowing for our students are connected with life in their homes and communities and the world. Children experience their own agency where their voices are heard in a climate of respect and recognition.

Our obligation as educators is to help our students become actively engaged as participating subjects in events. As Mr. Greg's classroom illustrates, an ideal way to help is to foster educative communities distinguished by inclusive relationships, reciprocally shared, where there is room for stories that don't match the mainstream view of society. Such education is in part a coming to know one another and learning how to confront each other critically, honestly, and with compassionate imagination.

To learn, to come to know in an educative community is learning and knowing about subject matter, about one another, and about ourselves. And this can be encouraged well in an educative community where dialogue is present, where there is consensus seeking, where creative conflict is not feared—where transformation, both personal and communal, is present. Such an educative community I have shared with you here is likely to allow our gaps of knowing and relating to one another to be held in creative tension, giving us the capacity to know each other and to heal the yearning we all carry with us for *a place where we can be who we are.* That is the only place where education worthy of the name can take place.

I spent two months with the third grade class at Wetland School. During my last week, Le came over and gave me a piece of paper he had been writing on. Perhaps he sensed I would be leaving soon. Or maybe he just wanted to share this with me. He was in the habit of bringing me a book to read to him almost every day I was in class. Somehow he would always have a book ready and maneuver close to me. Then before I could blink, there was a book in front of me and Le pointing to it saying, "Read it." I would do so. Today was different. Instead of a book, Le had a piece of paper with his printing on it. Mr. Greg had shown them how to do a sense poem. Le came over to where I was sitting and said, "For you. Read it." And I read his first poem aloud:

> I see the cars going by
> I hear the wind blo[w]ing
> I smell leaves
> I touch my sister
> I taste my food

And then he looked into my eyes and smiled brighter than the sun.

Notes

1 Michael Walzer, *Spheres of Justice: A Defense of Pluralism and Equality*. New York: Basic Books, 1983, 29.

2 Ibid., xiv.

3 Ibid., 3.

4 Lois Lowry, *The Giver,* Boston: Houghton Mifflin, 1993.

5 Michael Walzer, 319.

6 Ibid., 31.

7 Here Walzer is making a point of distinction between justice and different forms of tyranny. His point, which for me is the crux of membership, is that to ensure complex equality we need institutions where people feel they have a stake in them. The institutions, such as school, are a form of social good. 316–18 passim.

8 See Vivian Paley, *You Can't Say You Can't Play,* Cambridge, Mass.: Harvard University Press, 1992, and *Kwanzaa and Me*, Cambridge, Mass.: Harvard University Press, 1995. Both books are an exploration of membership in a classroom, where the implicit beliefs and attitudes of the children are made explicit through their stories and Paley's. Her notion of community is expansive and inclusive, where problems are posed by the children who work together to try to solve them in a caring relationship in what become, throughout the year, the basis for unifying experiences.

9 See Herbert Kohl's *I Won't Learn From You and Other Thoughts on Creative Maladjustment.* New York: The New Press, 1994, 32.

10 Maxine Greene.

11 Ibid., 32–43 passim.

12 Sharon Quint, *Schooling Homeless Children: A Working Model for America's Public Schools* New York: Teachers College Press, Columbia University, 1994, 133.

13 Ibid., 133.

14 Across this country, states are mandating learning standards that are frequently attached to proficiency tests or other high stakes exams that reductively measure what teachers teach and students "learn."

Epilogue

I end with a story my mother used to tell me as a little girl. Her parents came from Mexico and throughout my growing up I witnessed my family's exile from their customs, their language, their ways of understanding as they drifted out more and more into the public sphere of work. Resilient and doggedly determined to make a better life for themselves and their children, the Vargas family learned English—and made sure their children spoke it without the tell-tale accent—and learned how to act, dress, speak in ways to minimize their Chicana roots. My mother taught me well. I barely understand or speak Spanish. I am well educated. I have traveled to many countries all over the world. I am an accomplished musician. But within my heart still throbs the lessons from the long hours working side by side with my mother, her sisters, and cousins in the kitchen making tamales. I hear the soft syllables as my Nina tells me about her girlhood. I see my mother's elegant hands with her long, painted nails, so perfectly beautiful as I sit right next to her and she tells me this story, which I carry with me as I teach and work, and as I write:

> Shhh, let me tell you an old story about an ancient woman, *La Huesera*, the Bone Woman.
>
> Oh, yes, she is known by many names, but it is the very same woman who dwells in the desert alone, only stirring when one of God's creatures is lost or died. *La Huesera* roams the desert, always moving from here and there, looking for bones. When she finds them, she places the bones carefully in her apron. Yes, just like the one I wear when I make the tortillas. She is best at finding the bones of once living creatures, and once she begins, she does not stop searching until all the bones of *criaturas* are in her apron. Only then does she go back to her cave. And when she gets to her cave, she builds a fire, sits beside it and then begins to think of what song she will sing. When the inspiration comes, she lays out all the *criaturas'* bones and waves her gnarled, old hands slowly over them all. A low deep sound comes from down her throat. I always loved it when my mother made the soft, low sound that I could feel in her body as she hummed.

> The song swells and echoes in the mountains, weaving crescendo, decrescendo, and notes thick and thin over the wind. And as she sings, the first length of muscle and tendon appears on the bone, but still she sings. Then a pelt and the *criatura* begins to inhale the cool rush of clean air into its lungs. Still, it is not enough. *La Huesera* sings and sings and sings until finally it awakens completely. Her work is hard and long and lasts all night, yet as dawn comes she is singing in the silence. As the rays of the sun break forth from the sky, the *criatura* rises, its spirit quickened and open. Full of life, it bursts forth into freedom, into the world as its true self. And *La Huesera* goes out again to find new bones for her apron.

In an educative community, we are like *La Huesera,* bringing all our children together to help sing them to their world, free to be themselves. We cannot force awakening, but rather coax it with our singing. And our songs must change as our children change, each deserving her or his own variation. And as our song emerges, another begins, until soon our children recognize their own song and the songs of the others and know through this their kinship.

References

Bateson, Mary Catherine. *Peripheral Vision: Learning Along the Way.* New York: HarperCollins, 1994.

Bruner, Jerome. *Acts of Meaning.* Cambridge, Mass.: Harvard University Press, 1990.

Buber, Martin. *Between Man and Man.* Translated by Roland Gregor Smith. New York: Collier Books, 1965.

Dewey, John. *Democracy and Education.* Carbondale, Ill.: Southern Illinois University Press, 1916/1985.

———. *Art and Experience.* New York: Perigree Books, 1934.

———. *Experience and Education.* Kappa Delta Pi Lecture Series. New York: Collier Books, 1963.

———. *How We Think.* Buffalo, New York: Prometheus Books, 1991.

Dickens, Charles. *Hard Times.* New York: Penguin Books, 1854/1980.

Egan, Kieran. *Primary Understanding.* New York: Routledge, 1988.

Friere, Paolo. *Pedagogy of the Oppressed.* New York: Continuum, 1970.

Frye, Northrup. *The Educated Imagination.* Bloomington: Indiana University Press, 1964.

Gallas, Karen. *The Languages of Learning: How Children Talk, Write, Dance, Draw and Sing Their Understanding of the World.* New York: Teachers College Press, 1994.

Greene, Maxine. *Releasing the Imagination: Essays on Education, the Arts, and Social Change.* San Francisco: Jossey-Bass, 1995.

Karp, Ivan, Christine Mullen Dreamer, and Steven D. Lavine. *Museums and Communities: The Politics of Public Culture.* Washington, D.C.: Smithsonian Institution Press, 1992.

Kohl, Herbert R. *I Won't Learn From You and Other Thoughts on Creative Maladjustment*. New York: The New Press, 1994.

Kozol, Jonathan. *Death at an Early Age*. New York: Penguin Books, 1967.

Lowry, Lois. *The Giver*. Boston: Houghton Mifflin, 1993.

McGuire, Margrit. *Storypath*. Chicago: Everyday Learning, 1996.

Meier, Deborah. *The Power of Their Ideas: Lessons for America from a Small School in Harlem*. Boston: Beacon Press, 1995.

Neusner, Jacob. *Telling Tales: Making Sense of Christian and Judaic Nonsense: The Urgency and Basis for Judeo-Christian Dialogue*. Louisville, Ky.: John Knox Press, 1993.

Nussbaum, Martha. *Love's Knowledge*. New York: Oxford University Press, 1990.

Paley, Vivian Gussin. *The Boy Who Would Be a Helicopter*. Cambridge, Mass.: Harvard University Press, 1990.

———. *You Can't Say You Can't Play*. Cambridge, Mass.: Harvard University Press, 1992.

———. *Kwanzaa and Me*. Cambridge, Mass.: Harvard University Press, 1995.

Palmer, Parker. *To Know As We Are Known*. Harper: San Francisco. 1993.

Paterson, Katherine. *A Sense of Wonder: On Reading and Writing Books for Children*. New York: Plume Books, 1995.

Polakow, Valerie. *Lives on the Edge: Single Mothers and Their Children in the Other America*. Chicago: University of Chicago Press, 1992.

Quint, Sharon. *Schooling Homeless Children: A Working Model for America's Public Schools*. New York: Teachers College Press, 1994.

Romano, Rosalie. "How Do Experienced Teachers Learn New Strategies for Teaching?" Unpublished case study of Steve Bell's Storyline Workshop, University of Washington, 1992.

Walzer, Michael. *Spheres of Justice: A Defense of Pluralism and Equality*. New York: Basic Books, 1983.

Appendix A

Storyline As Critical Teaching

What is worth experiencing and learning? How do we help our students learn in meaningful and memorable ways? Such questions are present in the minds of caring teachers whenever they begin the school year or meet a new class. To address these questions for his students, Mr. Greg chose Storyline, a method that is used widely across the world since its inception in Scotland over thirty years ago. What are the principles of this method that foster student engagement, critical awareness and thinking, and powerful understandings? And how can a curriculum and instruction foster an educative community?

As I illustrated in this book, an educative community is predicated upon relations of trust. This is a crucial means of forging an educative community within one's classroom, regardless of who makes up the class or where it is. This trust in an educative community is a radically mutual relationship with people, particularly those who differ from us. Urban or rural, high or low socioeconomic level, majority or minority, young or old, the aim of education is to cultivate in each of our students critical thinking, public participation, and a strong notion of one's humanity. We teachers must be committed to work with our students wherever or whomever they are. How do we honor voices different from our own? This is our work in forging an educative community.

We must seek, as Sharon Thornton states, "a set of mutually engaged practices that lead to personal and public transformation toward more just and compassionate communities." Thornton beseeches us to seek an "honest and humble way to recognize others." This means we must listen to our students with absolute respect for their agency, for who they are and what they bring with them. Through trust we can discover respect that is "pro-active and involves the willingness to make a commitment to the deep humanness of [our students]."[1] Trust and respect must be the foundation for our work that is connected to and a part of what we are to "teach" (e.g. literacy of reading, writing, etc.) our students in our classrooms. Such relations can constitute an educative community. But can curriculum and instruction foster an educative community?

Before we can answer that question, we must ask what it is that we want to do with our students. If we want to reach our students, then we must ask about how they make sense of ideas and experiences, new and old. Kieran Egan writes about the story form, and claims that human beings are lovers of story and the story form.[2] Teachers know this: our students resonate with a good story. Story helps us all, including our students, make sense of the world.

Let's think about story more particularly and critically for our purposes. We use story in our classrooms, frequently without much thought. Stories can invite our students' interest, so we use it to help elucidate a topic or arouse curiosity about a topic or simply to serve our imagination about a topic. We think about story as a group of facts and actions and imagination in a narrative structure, with a plot that involves characters, episodes and incidents. We read stories to our students, or have them read stories, tell stories, write stories. But I want you to think in a different way about story right now, in a more critical way, using the metaphor of architecture, the art of construction and design.

Story is an architecture, with its foundation, walls, roof, and other structural pieces that create its design. Most of us use stories after they are designed, styled by whatever characters, plot and place that the story portrays. That's why story is such a powerful vehicle for all of us, including our students. We all "know" story's structure. There's predictability and inevitability about the way a story moves along, even though we may not know what will happen at the end. Whatever the plot, a powerful story will have cohesion and coherence in the interweaving of narrative plots.

If we were to choose story as a model for education, we could view ourselves and our students as architects, using the principles of structure to become producers of a design (style) and perspectives (characters) within a place (topic). Emerging from the design and perspective is ambiguity. (Recall that I argued how ambiguity can actually promote a social and intellectual space to enlarge our perceptions and differences. Otherwise, we might succumb to thinking that everyone agrees with us, or miss opportunities to invite multiple interpretations of a single event or episode.) When we think about using a story form as a model for education, we open up our classroom to ambiguity and contradictions and interpretation. These attributes are essential to becoming critical thinkers. Story form, then, can help us teach in ways that foster an educative community of critical thinkers.

If Storyline uses story as a model for education, then how is it structured and guided? The development of a Storyline around a topic is guided by the following:

- The topic is related to the conceptual development of students. It has epistemological complexity, focuses on a specific situation and creates a rich context that can include a variety of learning activities.
- Storyline is a collaboration of narrative sequence (guided as such by the teacher's key questions, e.g. What does your homeless character carry with him or her?)
- Storyline is moved forward by and dependent upon the students' characters' responses to the teacher's key questions.
- Each Storyline question, key and subsequent leading questions, relates to the particular episode of the narrative.
- Each episode (designated by key questions) has infinite potential in terms of possible development and investigation.
- The greater the collaboration between the students, the stronger the sense of ownership. The teacher does not tell the students what to do next. Nor does the teacher correct a student. Through negotiation and collaboration, it is the students themselves who come to understand the complexity of a topic and seek to make sense of their evolving understanding,

Let's talk about these basic principles of story as a model for education. This makes sense if we want to link our classrooms with the world, for story is a powerful model for reality that calls for interpretation, use of imagination and knowledge and experiences. Within a story lies conflict, surface and embedded conflicts that speak to our human condition; conflicts that deal with fears or safety, right or wrong, justice and injustice, knowing and not knowing, etc., causing us the reader to search for meaning within the plot. Values of what is good and what is not good are the invisible threads of any story, as the reader and narrator engage in the telling and the interpreting. Therefore, when we choose to use the story model for teaching, we can be like architects paying attention to outward and hidden structural designs.

An architect must understand the principles of design to create new and functional buildings that people can use. These buildings are public, in that we all see them. When story is used as a model for teaching, we are all involved and participating in structuring the world outside of our classroom. Storyline is one method that uses story as a model. We have talked about the basic principle of story as a vehicle for our students' making meaning. Before moving on to the other Storyline principles, let's talk about Storyline as an architectural device for education.

Storyline is an approach to curriculum integration (the history is told later in this appendix). Using story as a model, this method creates a context for curriculum linkage through the study of a topic. (Note: The outline of the Homeless Storyline Mr Greg follows is at the end of this appendix along with a biography sheet and Storyline references.) We saw how Mr. Greg used the topic of homelessness, a social issue in our society, to help his students not only come to understand the complexity of what it means to be homeless, but to link literacy of reading, writing, and speaking to thinking and negotiation skills, participation and interpretation among students with differing perspectives.

Storyline is built upon the essential elements of a story, and it is created in a collaboration between students, each episode guided by a conceptual question, e.g. Mr. Greg begins the Storyline with "What do you think of when you hear the word "homeless?" Place or setting of a particular time in the homeless Storyline began in a park near the third graders' school, but then moved out into the city, and, eventually, across the Pacific Ocean to Japan. People or characters in the homeless Storyline were the people created by the students, who represented their generalizations, stereotypes and conceptual understanding of homeless people through their Storyline characters. Through the homeless Storyline, the students were guided to reflect on what it means to live a life, and in particular, a life of homelessness.

Storyline is created by the students and represents their initial and subsequent understandings of a topic over the course of the topic study. Mr. Greg's students had gone through a one month Storyline at the start of the year. Do you remember how many of the students still referred back to that first Storyline? The homeless Storyline lasted about six weeks long, with an hour being set aside at least three times a week. Storyline fits into the routine of classrooms. In Scotland, teachers use basic skill work in the mornings and Storyline in the afternoon. There is no "official" length of time for any Storyline. It is the teacher who sets the direction through guiding questions, and the students who collaborate together through their characters to respond to those questions. Storyline teachers adapt this method to their schedule. I have used it in self contained classrooms, in my middle school block scheduled classrooms, and with my university students who may meet only once or twice a week. We'll talk about this sense of ownership and engagement in a few minutes.

Everyone is a part of Storyline because it requires all the characters (and their student creators) to collaboratively design and then build on one another's story. A Storyline sustains, then, multiple perspectives, and, because there cannot be just one point of view, the Storyline is much like an adventure for participants. They don't know what tomorrow will bring! Yet there is no insecurity or anxiety about not knowing, because Storyline is structured on a familiar model of the narrative. Students don't know what will happen next, but as they work through their collaboration, a sense of anticipation emerges. This anticipation comes out of their involvement in the story they are creating together. Their individual perspectives about a topic, like homelessness, are woven into their characters' lives. When a new understanding or idea is thought of, their characters' ideas and perspectives can adopt or change it to suit their context. Whatever happens, students will try to make sense of it. At some time or another during the Storyline, the third graders challenged some of their classmates' characters. Sometimes it was on a person's age and how it was that they could be a homeless baby and take care of itself. Do you recall when students were so puzzled by a character being "older than the universe?" How old is our universe anyway, and how can one be older than it? In a deeper sense, this principle of ownership encourages responsibility for their own ideas. When invited to make decisions and act upon them through their characters, students learn to become critical, yet respectful. What if that character is right about a point? Am I sure of my belief?

This social construction of understanding is supported by the principle of context. Nothing happens in a Storyline, regardless of the topic, without there being a context from which the characters and their creators can refer to. Even in the homeless Storyline, while there was no mural of place to put their characters, the context was the homelessness itself. Students continually had to explain a situation about their character or struggle with not having a place to sleep or to safely store belongings. The context was the struggle to exist in a society that has no place for those without jobs or homes. This was always in the mind of the students whose characters were worried about the police or being mugged.

In Storyline, the context of a topic is collaboratively created through a frieze or mural on the wall. The characters build their homes and communities on this frieze, constructed by the students who work together to respond to a key question "What does____ look like? What things do we need to add to our frieze to make it look like ______?" Each time Storyline has an episode, students must build on what they had done prior. Sometimes this means looking more critically at one's work and changing it. This evolving knowledge culture creates an insistent need to know for students. When Nino was figuring out the shape of his character's eyes, there was intense concentration to determine how an eye is shaped. Each new activity the students undertook called for them to step back and notice or remember. Such reflection, while internal for many of us, is shared between the character's creators, which leads to more complex reflection and awareness.

Through joint collaboration on a Storyline, students are asked to make decisions through their characters. These decisions are made but they are subject to change (or veto, if one's partner disagrees). Mr. Greg asked a key question to the homeless characters, What is it like living on the streets? The answers the characters gave at first were more obvious to the students. But each day new information was brought into the classroom to share with everyone. News articles, a talk show program on radio, a program on TV, and more were shared by some of the students each day. As such, their responses to What is it like living on the streets? became more complicated as more information was learned. In many classrooms, when teachers and students embark on a study of a topic, the teacher brings in speakers, videos, and an assortment of references to share with students *prior* to their beginning work on the topic. In Storyline, whatever the topic, the opposite approach is taken. When a resource person is invited to share with the students toward the end of a Storyline, the speaker, like Ashley Conder, is surprised by the level of questions and discussion from students. They, too, have something to share with the speaker. The visit takes the form of a discussion, not as an expert coming in to lecture on some topic.

The principle of prior understanding is part of what a Storyline teacher builds on when a topic is begun. The Storyline teacher wants students to begin to notice and look with more critical eyes, to notice what might have been there all along. Therefore, Storyline begins with key questions that query what students already know or can think of about any given topic. "What comes to mind when I say homeless?" And the students told him, though they were savvy to Mr. Greg, remembering his lectures and the discussions in the fall about how they treated the homeless in the park. Even so, their responses to his key question, offered modestly and openly after Le joined the class, gave insight into deeper beliefs about homeless people.

Collaborative storymaking must build upon experiences of students first. Teachers have to know what the students already understand about a topic, especially, when it is in error. And, this is tough for many of us, we do not correct at this point. We listen and mark down on chart sheets to be placed around the room with each new question. This way, students make public what they think, and also, as the Storyline progresses, it is inevitable to see the students mark out or revise a list. Corrections and amendments occur as students learn more about the topic. Because all work is public and shared, students become cultural critics about their context, challenging, as Peter did so well, and forcing all participants to reflect and reconsider.

This process of asking, posting publicly, amending and revising provides a structure that students build upon through their writing and reading, and all their other work in Storyline. The work itself becomes meaningful for students, and, no longer fragmented and empty, there is a desire to complete the work because they have to introduce their character and must be ready with the biography, or their journal must be accurate because it is to be read and included in the class reader book.

Whatever the level of skills the student has, there is a clear understanding between a Storyline teacher and students that the students can and do think for themselves. Students' realities are not ignored or buried, but welcomed and honored in Storyline. Letters written by students are read aloud and placed in a class book, so one can go back and reference a particular entry.

Many students in Mr. Greg's classroom were not fluent in English or were not fluent readers and writers. Through Storyline with its context that students could draw from and with the social construction of understandings always in play, Mr. Greg, and other Storyline teachers attend to structure that will support students in their learning. The journals the students wrote eventually became their basal readers and compiled as a class book. How did Mr. Greg adjust for the wide range of skills in his classroom? When it came time to begin the journal, he wove key questions into the introduction to structure it for the students. "If I look at a piece of writing, how would I know it is a journal?" "What is the difference between a journal entry and a report you have written?" These and other questions gave students not only some structure for what Mr. Greg was asking them to do, but also provided opportunity to share with everyone in the class their concept of what a journal entry was. The students reflected on each answer and Mr. Greg demonstrated on a large flip chart sheet what the structure of a journal entry looked like, its purpose, and what the content might be. All these characteristics were under the direction of the students, and even if you did not join in, any student could see an example of what was being asked. The date went at the upper right hand corner. The name of the character went under the date, and so forth.

Whenever journal entries were scheduled to be read aloud, all were treated with respect. Each student was an author and listened to other authors attentively. All journal entries were read by their authors each week, then compiled into the class book so anyone could go back and read past entries. Since the journals were written from the point of view of the characters, everyone had a stake in what was being read, since one experience could be understood by one character in an entirely different way than another. When a weapon was revealed as part of a homeless character's arsenal, journal entries for that week were commentaries on the danger or necessity of owning guns. The students wrote their journals from their characters' perspectives, and many struggled with their own belief system that guns were highly dangerous for anyone to carry. The situations of some of the homeless characters mediated some students's personal beliefs about guns, prompting complex and often contradictory reflections in their writing. These were read aloud and the ideas became the catalyst for ongoing discussion and debate about gun laws and the right to bear arms. The students had caught a glimpse of the complexity of an issue because their characters had been pushed out of fear and vulnerability by their homeless state to carry a gun. Not every homeless character chose to do so, and this added to the deepening understanding of this complicated issue of gun control. Out of these debates came fresh understandings about what it means to be human and lead a life.

The richness of the homeless Storyline carried with it opportunities for inclusion of all students at whatever skill level they were. Everyone and each character were a part of this community, some homeless and some not. Many students commented or gave indications of a developed sense of appreciation for their own home, something most of us take for granted. Their appreciation was deepened by their daily imaginings of what life would bring their homeless character this day. Imagination of have not converged with imagination of have, and a compassionate imagination grew from this. When the disaster of the earthquake in Kobe, Japan left so many people homeless, the students did not need to see images on TV or hear descriptions of homes destroyed and families out on the streets of Kobe. They knew. They *knew.* And they acted as they could, through the organization of a food/supply drive.

This actually is an interesting event because the students did not develop the food drive plan on their own. They contacted the Japanese

Embassy in the city to ask what was needed by the earthquake victims. This was not a flash of sympathy, a flurry of activity, and a fast feel good act of sending something to the victims. The students reflected first and asked what exactly could they do to help and what would help the victims. They checked with the embassy and then proceeded to organize the drive, which was hugely successful. A connection between those homeless in Kobe and their characters (and themselves, too) had been forged so the response became strong and honest, and with understanding of the relatedness of all who struggle to live each day, homeless or not.

At this time in education, teachers are increasingly called to show how their teaching meets the standards. They are held to some distant organization's notion of accountability through proficiency tests and the like. The result too often is a narrowing and further fragmentation of what is taught and how it is taught, leaving teachers and students vulnerable. In many ways, as reductive lessons are forced upon teachers to "increase test scores" the opportunity to teach in contextually rich and intellectually stimulating projects like Storyline seem to be lost. Yet, we must not lose heart, nor begin to doubt what we know our students need and long for — meaningful learning, an awareness of purpose, and new ways of thinking and being in the world. While too many of us and of our students no longer remember this need and longing, I can assure you that when you experience involvement in teaching and learning like the homeless Storyline example, you do not forget it. I tell my students that when you are in a class that forges an educative community, with relations of trust, a power of understanding, with compassionate imagination and a sense of belonging, you are "ruined" — ruined to sit through grill, drill and kill assignments, empty of content and context. I say this, because the origins of Storyline grew out of a time in Scotland not unlike our own right now, with national standards and testing that forced reorganization of the curriculum.

The History of Storyline

The Storyline Method,[3] sometimes known as Storypath in the United States,[4] was developed in Scotland during a period of school reform. A revision of the national curriculum left classroom teachers adrift in new standards and restructured curriculum expectations. "The Primary Memorandum" was published by the Scottish Education Department in 1965, recommending that the subjects studied in primary school should be integrated. As traditionally separated subjects (e.g., English, history, mathematics, science, etc.) were consolidated into five umbrella categories of language, mathematics, environmental studies, expressive arts, and religious, social, and moral education, it became evident to teachers that the reform meant more than just teaching different subjects. It meant teaching subjects differently. Traditional instructional approaches were called into question as it became increasingly evident to teachers that such approaches could not meet the new standards that included integration of topics.

In 1967, a Staff Tutor Team of three lecturers was appointed by Jordanhill College of Education (now the Faculty of Education at Strathclyde University). Its function was to help teachers to structure and plan this new area of integrated curriculum known as environmental studies. Bill Michael, Fred Rendell and Steve Bell were the original members, but shortly after they were formed, Bill Michael left and his place was taken by Sallie Harkness. Over the following years with the help of countless teachers, headteachers and advisors, Storyline was developed. Steve and Sallie are still working as Storyline Consultants. The flexibility of the approach has meant that it has been adopted by teachers in many different countries. At a recent meeting of the European Association for Educational Design, an international seminar for Storyline Educators, over ten countries around the world were represented.

In 1989, Storyline was brought to the United States by Kathy Fifield, a Portland, Oregon teacher (now deceased) who had discovered it while on a Fulbright in the United Kingdom. Fifield left a legacy of Storyline throughout the west coast of the US where she organized Storyline workshops for teachers in schools from Washington state to California. When she died, she left her consultancy, Storyline Design, to two colleagues, Jeff Creswell, Portland, Oregon, and Eileen Vopelak, Santa Barbara, California, who are carrying on the work she started.

The following year, Margit McGuire, Chair of Teacher Education at Seattle University, while attending a conference in Germany independently learned about Storyline and saw its application for American education. Her work with teachers, both pre- and in-service, has now made Storyline (which she termed Storypath) a part of a number of school curricula throughout the U.S.

In 1990, Professor McGuire invited Steve Bell to give a course at Seattle University. I was one of the educators present at this first Storyline course. This book came out of my participation in that and subsequent institutes, where I began analyzing Storyline's unwritten underlying principles and conducting observational research.[5]

Storyline, according to McGuire,[6] is an approach to organizing the curriculum as well as an instructional strategy. It assumes that children learn and are engaged when they are active participants in their own learning, placing them in the center of the educational enterprise. The structure of Storyline provides external parameters, but internal space to explore topics and discover connections with their own lives. From such a combination comes meaning-making and the potential for powerful, motivating educational experiences.

Storyline is built upon the components of story, a primary way humans come to make sense of the world. Each Storyline unit becomes a story that provides a concrete context in which to develop understanding of social science content and affords natural opportunities to develop and use basic skills. Stories engage children. They anticipate what will happen next, and work at bringing all the threads of the plot together to make sense.

Each Storyline unit begins by introducing a setting for the story and creating characters for the story. Such a context provides both teacher and students opportunities to draw throughout the Storyline. When students are confronted with critical incidents, their responses arise out of what they know of the context, the characters, and what has gone on before. As each critical incident is introduced and problem solved by the students, an ever complex plot emerges that keeps children engaged and involved.

Throughout each Storyline, students negotiate and collaborate together in a variety of groupings, from working alone, with a partner, or with different sizes of groups. In this way, students eventually come to work with everyone, getting to know each other as well as the characters. Working together, students try to problem solve issues raised through the critical incidents. These critical incidents come in the form of questions a teacher asks, such as, What do you think of when I say homelessness? Or How would a homeless person carry his or her belongings? The more a teacher probes, the more the children contribute, providing the teacher with ways to guide them to new and deeper understandings. In this way, the teacher's role is to guide students toward this understanding as they acquire and construct new knowledge. Key questions in a Storyline should cause students to think more deeply or consider new ideas to problem solve, research, and investigate.

The structure of Storyline allows teachers to teach both process skills and content that are essential to established curriculum standards. The structure naturally integrates various subject matter disciplines along with reading and writing, listening and speaking, social studies, science and the arts. Both content and process skills are connected through the story form, fostering sense-making and engagement in students.

For those who have not heard of The Storyline Method, you will find website information at the end of this section, along with the outline for the Homeless Storyline.

We chose our profession of teaching to reach out to our students and help them become members of our society who are active participants and lead lives of connection and health. The commitment of teachers I meet who are seeking to help their students learn in memorable and meaningful ways is deep and abiding. Whenever I am in a group of such dedicated teachers, our conversation turns to sharing ways of helping our students learn. We share our stories of the classroom, both our successes and joys as well as our failures. We need our failures to help teach us how to teach, and this is never ending work. And our work is a moral endeavor, both in pushing ourselves to become better teachers as well as in helping our students realize their own agency, and therefore, their power of human possibility. I have never been sorry that I chose to teach. My journey continues as long as my courage stands.

In this time of testing frenzy and standardization, we must be intellectuals for one another and advocates for our students. We need to raise questions for every pressure to teach in a way that might reduce or empty the teaching act to meaninglessness. For whose benefit do we teach a certain way? How can we reach each of our students? Will an approach or instructional method support, foster, and encourage the full development of my students, both intellectually and socially? What do we honor in teaching if not the growth of our students? I maintain that if we attend only to some narrow cognitive measure then we will lose our children. Our children are telling us that something is wrong each time there is a school shooting or a student who drops out. How can we respond if we don't listen to our children?

As teachers, we are in positions of leadership; we only need to recognize how powerful our voices can be if we join together to advocate for our students. Forging an educative community in each of your classrooms takes commitment, for it begins in honoring our students for their richness of being. Forging an educative community, like our democracy, is dynamic and constantly being re-formed. We can shape the dispositions of our students to *want* to read, to write, to learn. We begin with our decision of who and what we honor.

Notes

1. Sharon Thornton, *Honoring Rising Voices: Pastoral Theology as Emancipatory Practice* unpublished essay 2000

2. Kieran Egan, *Primary Understanding :Education in Early Childhood*. New York, 1988. P 96–97

3. Margit E. McGuire, "Conceptual Learning in the Primary Grades, The Storyline Strategy," *Social Studies and the Young Learner*, 3(3), January /February 1991, 6–9; Ian M. Barr & Margit E. McGuire, "Social Studies and Effective Stories," *Social Studies and the Young Learner*, 5(3), January/February 1993, 6–8 ff.

4. Margit E McGuire, *Storypath* (Chicago: Everyday Learning, 1996).

5. Rosalie Romano, "How Do Experienced Teachers Learn New Strategies for Teaching?" Unpublished case study of Steve Bell's Storyline Workshop, University of Washington, 1992.

6. McGuire, *Storypath*.

Appendix B

The Homeless Storyline Outline

This is the Storyline Outline used for the Homeless Storyline in *Forging an Educative Community*. Note the parsimony of the outline. This allows for adding questions as you build on your students' knowledge and experience. Each episode of any Storyline is led by key questions. These questions are meant to call forth students' conceptual understandings of a topic. As more responses are collected on chart paper and posted in the room, students have a base upon which to change or challenge what is on the list. The story is constructed communally through the interactions between and amongst the Storyline characters each student creates. The biography sheet at the end of the Homeless Storyline outline can be revised for any topic. There are basic questions, such as name, address, birthdate and age, family history, etc, that also provide younger students with a standard schema for many forms used in institutions and government agencies.

Anticipation becomes a hallmark of a Storyline in action, as students become aware of complications and surprises. No one really knows what a character might do or say that will change the perspective of a topic. It is the teacher, however, who must keep the thread of the topic always on the horizon. Since Storyline is integrative, many ideas may converge at once, all interesting. The teacher uses the key questions to continually guide the students deeper into the topic, saving new knowledge and different questions for a parallel study at another time.

The story belongs to the students and the sense of ownership is quickly established. The teacher does not change or rearrange anything on the frieze or mural, nor amend in any way the students' characters. Contextual richness emerges as the questions continue to be asked and answered, raising more questions that lead to a web of interlocking ideas about the topic. This context is co-constructed by all the students and each character in response to the key questions the teacher asks. Within a short while, Storyline teachers realize they have doubled their class size, since they must know their students and each of the characters and each character's family history.

A major principle of Storyline is to allow the context and structure to grow and develop before any field trip or expert is called upon to share with the class about the topic. Usually reserved toward mid way or the last few weeks of a Storyline, the visit to a place or person (or having a guest visit the class) is a cause of great excitement and anticipation. The resultant exchange is no longer the students listening to an expert, but now there exists a spirited dialogue with questions students *want* to know the answers to and a guest speaker who is excited to share beyond the superficial aspects of the topic.

Storyline ends positively with a celebration or activity that accentuates the Storyline community and journey that was accomplished. Mr Greg ended with a poem of living, a recognition that life is on going and full of promise, even in the midst of uncertainty.

Storyline Information:
Steve Bell email: <steve@storyline-scotland.freeserve.co.uk>
Storyline Scotland Website: http://storyline-scotland.freeserve.co.uk
Rosalie Romano email: <storylinemethod@hotmail.com>
Storyline Education Website: http://www.oak.cats.ohiou/edu/~romano
West Coast Storyline Connection <storyline@teleport.com>
or <stryline@sbceo.org>

Topic Outline: The Homeless Storyline

Rosalie Romano and Douglas Selwyn

Storyline	Key Questions	Pupil Activity	Class Organization	Materials	Outcome Assessment
1. Homelessness	*What doe you think of when you have the word "homeless?"* *What does it mean to be homeless?* *What reasons are there for people to be homeless?*	Brainstorm/List	Individual Whole group	Chart Paper Markers Tape	Vocabulary Concept formation Perspective taking

* Storyline usually begins the collaborative construction of a mural or frieze of the location in which characters will live, including geographical and human made landscape. Because these characters are homeless, they must struggle and compete for any wall space within the classroom.

Topic Outline: The Homeless Storyline

Storyline	Key Questions	Pupil Activity	Class Organization	Materials	Outcome Assessment
2. The Homeless People	*Who are these homeless people?* *Are they young or old? Men, women, children?* *Are they of European American, African American, Asian American, Hispanic American, Native American, or other ethnics or racial ancestry?*	Brainstorm/lists Pairs create face of their homeless character (Approx. Size 8"X11") Teacher Demonstrates: Show outline of a face –ask what is missing? (have nose, eyes, hair etc. ready to glue) – students notice and discuss shapes of eyes, nose, face, ears, types of hair etc. Characters displayed on walls	Pairs	Scissors Construction paper of skin tone colors to represent wide variety of racial & ethnic backgrounds Glue sticks Markers Yarn Raw wool Remnants of fabric Arts & crafts material	Design skills Art technique Scale Proportion Perspective Vocabulary Negotiation Questioning Problem-solving Dialogue 3 dimensional art Awareness of physical characteristics of people

Topic Outline: The Homeless Storyline

Storyline	Key Questions	Pupil Activity	Class Organization	Materials	Outcome Assessment
3. Who Are the Homeless?	*What is your homeless character's name, age and birthdate, family background, height, weight?* *How did your character become homeless?* *Who are his/her friends? Pets? Hopes? Fears? Childhood memories? Favorite food? Music? Activities? (assure students they will add more as we all get to know their homeless characters)*	Brainstorm/List Create a biography of a homeless character Present & introduce character to class	Pairs Whole group Individual	Biography sheet Pen Pencil Tape	Logic computation Discussion Negotiation Oral presentation Questioning problem solving

Topic Outline: The Homeless Storyline

Storyline	Key Questions	Pupil Activity	Class Organization	Materials	Outcome Assessment
4. Our Homeless Community	*Why are these people homeless?* *Are other reasons other people might be homeless?* *Who are they?* *How do others treat them?* *How do they view their situation?*	Brainstorm/List Identify Commonalities Differences Write the story of how their character becomes homeless	Pairs Whole group	Chart Paper Tape Markers Chalk	Biographical writing Discrimin-ation analysis Narrative writing

Topic Outline: The Homeless Storyline

Storyline	Key Questions	Pupil Activity	Class Organization	Materials	Outcome Assessment
5. A Day in the Life of a Homeless Person	*What does your homeless character have to do to survive each day?* *What are the basic needs of a person?* *How does s/he meet those needs?* *What kinds of things might happen to a homeless person?*	Brainstorm/List Oral presentations Writing (descriptive, poetic) Map of area to show where your homeless character travels, lives, etc.	Pairs Whole group	Paper Pen Pencils Tape Chart paper Markers	Outlining Vocabulary Map reading Map making Narrative writing Descriptive writing Interpretation

Topic Outline: The Homeless Storyline

Storyline	Key Questions	Pupil Activity	Class Organization	Materials	Outcome Assessment
6. Finding Shelter	*Where does your homeless character spend the night?* *What are the obstacles & challenges to finding a place to sleep?*	Brainstorm/List Descriptive writing Draw the place where character spent last night	Whole group Pairs	Chart paper Markers Pencil Pen Paper	Descriptive writing Problem solving Oral presentation skills

Topic Outline: The Homeless Storyline

Storyline	Key Questions	Pupil Activity	Class Organization	Materials	Outcome Assessment
7. A Visit from A Social Worker	*What agencies (school, community, city, etc.) work to help the homeless?* *What things do we want to know?*	Brainstorm/List Interview a social worker	Whole group	Video player to show tape on agency work	Problem solving Compre-hension Problem-posing Questioning Synthesis Public action

Topic Outline: The Homeless Storyline

Storyline	Key Questions	Pupil Activity	Class Organization	Materials	Outcome Assessment
8. A Visit from a Homeless Person	*What was/is it like to be homeless?* *What things do we want to know?*	Brainstorm/List Interview a homeless person (teenager?)	Whole group	Paper Pen	Problem - solving Problem - posing Compre-hension Synthesis Analysis Public action Interpre-tation

Topic Outline: The Homeless Storyline

Storyline	Key Questions	Pupil Activity	Class Organization	Materials	Outcome Assessment
9. Awaking to a New Day	*What does your homeless character sense when the new day begins?*	Students close eyes & imagine their character is waking up in the morning. Imaging 3 things their character can see, then 3 things their character can touch, 3 things they can hear, 3 things they can taste & smell, and imagine the emotion their character feels.	Pairs Whole group	Paper Pen Pencils Tape	Poetry writing Metaphors Interpretation Recitation of Poem Display of poems

Topic Outline: The Homeless Storyline

Storyline	Key Questions	Pupil Activity	Class Organization	Materials	Outcome Assessment
9. Continued		I see… I hear… I taste… I smell… I touch… I feel… (emotion) Have students read their poems dropping the "I see… etc."			

BIOGRAPHY SHEET FOR YOUR STORYLINE CHARACTER

Name: ____________________ Age: __________

Date of birth: ________________ Place of birth: ________________

Distinguishing features: ____________________

Family members: ____________________

Personality characteristics: ____________________

How did your homeless character become homeless? ____________________

How are you treated by others? ____________________

What are you worried about? ____________________

What are your hopes for the future? ____________________

Who are your friends? Do you have pets? What do you like to eat? __________

Index

COUNTERPOINTS

Studies in the Postmodern Theory of Education

General Editors
Joe L. Kincheloe & Shirley R. Steinberg

Counterpoints publishes the most compelling and imaginative books being written in education today. Grounded on the theoretical advances in criticalism, feminism, and postmodernism in the last two decades of the twentieth century, Counterpoints engages the meaning of these innovations in various forms of educational expression. Committed to the proposition that theoretical literature should be accessible to a variety of audiences, the series insists that its authors avoid esoteric and jargonistic languages that transform educational scholarship into an elite discourse for the initiated. Scholarly work matters only to the degree it affects consciousness and practice at multiple sites. Counterpoints' editorial policy is based on these principles and the ability of scholars to break new ground, to open new conversations, to go where educators have never gone before.

For additional information about this series or for the submission of manuscripts, please contact:

Joe L. Kincheloe & Shirley R. Steinberg
637 West Foster Avenue
State College, PA 16801

To order other books in this series, please contact our Customer Service Department:

(800) 770-LANG (within the U.S.)
(212) 647-7706 (outside the U.S.)
(212) 647-7707 FAX

Or browse online by series:

www.peterlang.com